$\mathscr{P}$ ROFILES IN WORLD HISTORY

Significant Events and the People
Who Shaped Them

Volume 3: *The Crusades to Building Empires in the Americas, 1095-1500*

Crusades and Mongol Expansion
  Saladin, Genghis Khan, Innocent III, Alexius V
Religion and Reason in the Middle Ages
  Averroës, Maimonides, Thomas Aquinas
Beginning of Constitutional Government in England
  Thomas Becket, King John
Muslim Influences on Empires in West Africa
  Al-Bakri, Sundiata, Mansa Musa
Exploring the East
  Marco Polo, William of Rubrouck, Ibn Battutah
Building Empires in Europe and Asia
  Timur Lenk, Mehmed II, Ivan the Great, Babur
Building Empires in the Americas
  Topa Inca Yupanqui, Moctezuma I

Volume 4: *The Age of Discovery to Industrial Revolution, 1400-1830*

Beginnings of the Age of Discovery
  Cheng Ho, Vasco da Gama, Jacques Cartier
Religious Reform
  Desiderius Erasmus, Guru Nanak, Ignatius of Loyola, Martin Luther
Revival of Science
  Leonardo da Vinci, Tycho Brahe, Johannes Kepler
Revival of Literature
  Francis Bacon, Miguel de Cervantes, William Shakespeare
Rise of Nationalism
  Suleiman the Magnificent, Hideyoshi Toyotomi, Catherine the Great
Enlightenment
  John Locke, Voltaire, Jean-Jacques Rousseau
Industrial Revolution
  Charles Townshend, Richard Arkwright, James Watt

(Continued on inside back cover)

PROFILES IN
WORLD HISTORY

Social Reform to World Wars

1900
Sigmund Freud introduces psychoanalysis.

1903
Wilbur and Orville Wright make the first powered airplane flight.

1905
Civil war begins in Russia.

1907
Pablo Picasso introduces cubism.

1912
China's Manchu government is overthrown.

1914
World War I begins with the assassination of Archduke Ferdinand.

1917
Russian Revolution.

1918
Armistice ends World War I.

1919
Albert Einstein's theory of relativity is confirmed during a total eclipse.

1929
Western capitalism collapses in the Great Depression.

1933
Adolf Hitler takes control of the German government.

1939
World War II begins with Germany's invasion of Poland.

1945
Germany surrenders. U.S. drops atom bombs on Japan; Japan surrenders.

PROFILES IN WORLD HISTORY

Significant Events and the People

Who Shaped Them

Social Reform to World Wars

JOYCE MOSS

and

GEORGE WILSON

AN IMPRINT OF GALE RESEARCH
AN INTERNATIONAL THOMSON PUBLISHING COMPANY

PROFILES IN WORLD HISTORY
Significant Events and the People Who Shaped Them

VOLUME 6: SOCIAL REFORM TO WORLD WARS
Joyce Moss and George Wilson

Staff

Carol DeKane Nagel, *U•X•L Developmental Editor*
Julie L. Carnagie, *U•X•L Assistant Editor*
Thomas L. Romig, *U•X•L Publisher*

Shanna P. Heilveil, *Production Assistant*
Evi Seoud, *Assistant Production Manager*
Mary Beth Trimper, *Production Director*

Barbara A. Wallace, *Permissions Associate (Pictures)*

Mary Krzewinski, *Cover and Page Designer*
Cynthia Baldwin, *Art Director*

Graphix Group, *Typesetting*

Library of Congress Cataloging-in-Publication Data

Profiles in World History : the people who shaped significant events / edited by Joyce Moss and George Wilson.
   p. cm.
   Includes bibliographical references and index
   Summary: Each chapter focuses on one particular event which is placed in historical context and followed by
      biographical profiles of individuals who played active roles in the event.
   ISBN 0-7876-0464-X (set : acid-free paper). — ISBN 0-7876-0465-8 (v. 1 : acid-free paper). — ISBN 0-7876-0466-6
      (v. 2 : acid-free paper). — ISBN 0-7876-0467-4 (v. 3 . acid-free paper). — ISBN 0-7876-0468-2 (v. 4 : acid-free
      paper). — ISBN 0-7876-0469-0 (v. 5 : acid-free paper). — ISBN 0-7876-0470-4 (v. 6 : acid-free paper). —
      ISBN 0-7876-0471-2 (v. 7 : acid-free paper). — ISBN 0-7876-0472-0 (v. 8 : acid-free paper).
   1. World history—Juvenile literature. 2. Biography—Juvenile literature. [1. World history. 2. Biography.] I.
      Moss, Joyce, 1951–. II. Wilson, George, 1920–.
D21.P94 1996
909—dc20

                           95–41611
                              CIP
                              AC

∞™ This book is printed on acid-free paper that meets the minimum requirements of American National Standard for Information Sciences—Permanence Paper for Printed Library Materials, ANSI Z39.48-1984.

Printed in the United States of America

10 9 8 7 6 5 4 3 2

Contents

Social Reform 1

Science Exploring the Unseen World 30

Expanding Global Communications 72

Twentieth-Century Revolutions 104

Experimentation in the Arts 140

World Wars 170

Reader's Guide

Profiles in World History: Significant Events and the People Who Shaped Them presents the life stories of more than 175 individuals who have played key roles in world history. The biographies are clustered around 50 broad events, ranging from the Rise of Eastern Religions and Philosophies to the Expansion of World Powers, from Industrial Revolution to Winning African Independence. Each biography—complete in itself—contributes a singular outlook regarding an event; when taken as cluster, the biographies provide a variety of views and experiences, thereby offering a broad perspective on events that shaped the world.

Those whose stories are told in *Profiles in World History* meet one or more of the following criteria. The individuals:

- Represent viewpoints or groups involved in a major world event
- Directly affected the outcome of the event
- Exemplify a role played by common citizens in that event

Format

Profiles in World History volumes are arranged by chapter. Each chapter focuses on one particular event and opens with an overview and detailed time line of the event that places it in historical context. Following are biographical profiles of two to five diverse individuals who played active roles in the event.

Each biographical profile is divided into four sections:

- **Personal Background** provides details that predate and anticipate the individual's involvement in the event

- **Participation** describes the role played by the individual in the event and its impact on his or her life

- **Aftermath** discusses effects of the individual's actions and subsequent relevant events in the person's life

- **For More Information** provides sources for further reading on the individual

Additionally, sidebars containing interesting details about the events and individuals profiled are interspersed throughout the text.

Additional Features

Portraits, illustrations, and maps as well as excerpts from primary source materials are included in *Profiles in World History* to help bring history to life. Sources of all quoted material are cited parenthetically within the text, and complete bibliographic information is listed at the end of each biography. A full bibliography of scholarly sources consulted in preparing each volume appears in each book's back matter.

Cross references are made in the entries, directing readers to other entries within the volume that are connected in some way to the person under scrutiny. Additionally, each volume ends with a subject index, while Volume 8 concludes with a cumulative subject index, providing easy access to the people and events mentioned throughout *Profiles in World History*.

Comments and Suggestions

We welcome your comments on this work as well as your suggestions for individuals to be featured in future editions of *Profiles in World History*. Please write: Editors, *Profiles in World History*, U·X·L, 835 Penobscot Bldg., Detroit, Michigan 48226-4094; fax to 313-961-6348; or call toll-free: 1-800-877-4253.

Acknowledgments

The editors would like to thank the many people involved in the preparation of *Profiles in World History*.

For guidance in the choice of events and personalities, we are grateful to Ross Dunn, Professor of History at the University of California at San Diego, and David Smith, Professor of History at California Polytechnic University at Pomona. We're thankful to Professor Smith for his careful review of the entire series and his guidance toward key sources of information about personalities and events.

We deeply appreciate the writers who compiled data and contributed to the biographies: Diane Ahrens, Bill Boll, Quesiyah Ali Chavez, Charity-Jean Conklin, Mario Cutajar, Craig Hinkel, Hillary Manning, Lawrence Orr, Phillip T. Slattery, Colin Wells, and Susan Yun. We'd especially like to thank Jamie Mohn and Cheryl Steets for their careful attention to the manuscript.

Thanks also to the copy editors and proofreaders, Sonia Benson, Barbara C. Bigelow, Betz Des Chenes, Robert Griffin, Rob Nagel, and Paulette Petrimoulx, for their careful attention to style and detail. Special thanks to Margaret M. Johnson, Judith Kass, and John F. Petruccione for researching the illustrations and maps.

And, finally, thanks to Carol Nagel of U·X·L for overseeing the production of the series.

Picture Credits

The photographs and illustrations appearing in *Profiles in World History: Significant Events and the People Who Shaped Them,* Volume 6: *Social Reform to World Wars* were received from the following sources:

On the cover: **The Granger Collection:** Igor Stravinsky, Emmeline Pankhurst; **The Bettmann Archive:** Sun Yat-sen.

AP/Wide World Photos: pp. 41, 66, 106, 116, 117, 142, 153, 159, 201, 209; **Archive Photos:** pp. 23, 60; **The Bettmann Archive:** p. 49; **The Granger Collection:** pp. 13, 15, 18, 28, 35, 37, 45, 46, 79, 82, 91, 95, 109, 112, 123, 125, 137, 163, 167, 174, 177, 179, 181, 212, 216; **Library of Congress:** p. 55; **The Metropolitan Museum of Art, Bequest of Gertrude Stein, 1946:** p. 155; **UPI/Bettmann:** pp. 63, 69, 77, 87, 99, 100, 121, 131, 135, 145, 150, 173, 189, 195, 199.

Social Reform

1882
▼
Baroness **Bertha von Suttner** begins writing about social reforms.

1883
▼
Beginning of social welfare legislation in Germany.

1905
▼
Von Suttner receives Nobel Prize for peace. Revolution begins in Russia. Unrest in Morocco.

1903
▼
Emmeline Pankhurst organizes Women's Social and Political Union.

1895
▼
Russians invade Turkistan. Japan defeats China.

1906
▼
Rosa Luxemburg arrested for socialist political agitation.

1907
▼
Universal male voting rights effected in Austria.

1912
▼
Universal male voting rights effected in Italy.

1912-13
▼
Balkan wars.

1919
▼
Communist Party suppressed in Germany; Luxemburg killed by government troops.

1918
▼
Socialist Spartacus League revolts against German government.

1915
▼
Luxemburg imprisoned for inciting riots in Germany.

1914
▼
World War I begins.

SOCIAL
REFORM

The nineteenth century was a period of extraordinary social change and political conflict in Europe. The Industrial Revolution had begun in the mid-eighteenth century and was now at full throttle, changing the base of the production of wealth from agriculture to manufacturing and transforming societies in the process.

Rural areas, the cottage industries of which were formerly the centers of economic production, declined as water-, steam-, and electricity-powered machines greatly accelerated production. The new machines were best housed in large factories where the sources of power were readily available. Workers abandoned their farms and cottage production to flock to homes near the factories. Villages grew into towns and towns into cities as a new population of factory workers was created. The towns and cities were ill-prepared to handle the host of social problems these rapid population increases brought.

The changes resulting from the new industrialization fostered inventions such as the electric light and the telephone. They also brought people of great wealth, particularly factory owners, into close contact with the poorly paid and overworked class of factory workers. This created a climate of tension and despair for those who did not share in the wealth, though there was hope that the added production would result in better conditions for everyone.

Industrialization created a demand for more raw materials and for new markets. Throughout Europe, competition among countries for shares in the new industrial wealth, along with the inability to resolve historical grudges, resulted in almost constant skirmishes between and within nations. European explorers were sent out to find new resources and markets; a scramble for control of Africa and Asia deepened conflicts between the great European powers.

Questioning the old order. Early in the twentieth century, men had claimed their rights to participate in the new governments; men achieved universal voting rights in Austria in 1907 and in Italy in 1912. A hundred years earlier, Mary Wollstonecraft had begun the call for equal rights for women in her *Vindication of the Rights of Women* (c. 1795). Throughout the nineteenth century, this call had been overshadowed by the need and demand for social reforms to aid both men and women struggling to adjust to the new industrial society. Social welfare legislation began in the first industrialized nation, Great Britain, and had spread to Germany by 1883.

By the beginning of the twentieth century, however, women were taking a different and stronger position as they sought a voice in government and society. **Emmeline Pankhurst** was an early leader in social reform, particularly in pressing for the rights of women. In 1903 she organized the Women's Social and Political Union. Individually and through this union, she carried on the crusade for women's rights for the rest of her life, eventually seeing voting rights for women and the right of women to run for Parliament in her native England.

Armed conflict among nations, however, was perhaps the dominant concern at the end of the nineteenth century. In this atmosphere an Austrian baroness, daughter of a field marshal in the Austrian army, devoted her life to advancing the cause of peace. Baroness **Bertha von Suttner** had seen wars arise over and over—between her own Austria and Germany in 1866 and between France and Prussia in 1870. A gifted writer, she rejected war as a means of settling international disputes and took up her pen to write a number of books championing world peace. Her work laid the foundations for the establishment of international institutions, such as the League of Nations, dedicated to the promotion of peace and international stability.

Polish-born **Rosa Luxemburg,** on the other hand, placed political and social reform before peace. She believed that only outright revolution would bring equality to people repressed by the governments that controlled wealth throughout Europe. She was a fervent believer in Marxist socialism, an economic philosophy and political movement named for German social theorist Karl Marx, which aims to achieve a just, classless society through public ownership and operation of the means of production and distribution of goods. Luxemburg helped found or was active in socialist parties in several European countries, wrote numerous articles and speeches in support of the socialist cause, and spent years in prison for her activities. After organizing Germany's first communist party, she was killed by troops serving the government she hoped to replace with a socialist system.

Bertha von Suttner

1843-1914

Personal Background

Noble outcasts. The Baroness Bertha von Suttner was born Countess Bertha Kinsky in Prague (then part of Austria, now in the Czech Republic) in June 1843. Her family descended from the House of Kinsky, a noble line of Austrian counts.

The family had enough money to see that Bertha received the finest education available to a young woman. Still, Bertha and her mother could not directly trace sixteen forebears to the House of Kinsky, and thus they did not pass the strict test for entrance and full social acceptance into Austrian noble society. The status of outcast wounded Bertha; she would bitterly remember those days in her later writings, which included withering critiques of the aristocracy.

It was abroad that Bertha and her mother gained the social acceptance among the European aristocracy that they had been denied in Austria. The Kinskys lived several years in Paris, Rome, and other international capitals. Bertha acquired fluency in a number of European languages and made contacts that would serve her well in her later years of political activism and diplomacy.

In 1876, after her mother had gambled away the family fortune, Bertha and her mother returned to Austria, where Bertha took a governess position with the family of Baron von Suttner.

▲ Bertha von Suttner

Event: Leading the peace movement.

Role: The work of writer Bertha von Suttner laid the foundations for the establishment of international institutions aimed at maintaining peace and stability in Europe and throughout the world. Von Suttner was also instrumental in convincing Swedish chemist and philanthropist Alfred Nobel to establish the Nobel Peace Prize, which recognized pioneers in the peace movement. Von Suttner was its first female recipient.

After working for nearly one year, she was recommended for and soon accepted a secretarial position with chemist and philanthropist Alfred Nobel in Paris. Though she was overcome with homesickness and returned to Austria less than a month later, it was the beginning of a long correspondence with the famed inventor of dynamite.

Marriage and the beginning of a literary career. In 1877, much to the surprise of the von Suttner family, Bertha eloped with their youngest son, Arthur, a man seven years her junior. The newlyweds made their way to Russia to stay with the Princess von Mingrelia, a friend from Bertha's Paris days. Arthur von Suttner was a known fiction writer by then, and for the first time, both he and Bertha had to work to support themselves. Bertha turned to writing as well and eventually established a reputation as an author. She wrote several novels of social criticism and published studies of important issues plaguing Europe. She also began a rigorous course of self-study, which laid the foundations for the peace campaigns she would soon lead.

The Kinskys

From her heritage, few would expect that Bertha von Suttner would become an activist for world peace. Her father was Austrian field marshal Franz Kinsky. He died while Bertha was still an infant. Bertha's mother, the Countess Kinsky, raised her daughter with the hope that the child would be recognized by Austrian high society. Countess Kinsky was descended from a long line of scholars that included the popular German poet Theodor Körner.

Participation: Leading the Peace Movement

Literature and politics. In 1885 the Baron and Baroness von Suttner returned to Austria to commence political activism to further a growing peace movement. For von Suttner, writing was the perfect vehicle for peace work. She became involved with a Munich periodical, *Die Gesellschaft,* published by a group of activists.

In addition to the journalism she pursued on behalf of *Die Gesellschaft,* in 1882 von Suttner began the first of several novels that continued her examination of the changing face of European society. Titled *High Life,* the work explores the issues of social progress and democracy. Its principle character, an American, compares life abroad to life in the States. *A Bad Lot, Daniela Dormes,* and *Before the Storm* followed, all addressing important social topics of the day.

A second meeting with Nobel. The von Suttners' writing financed long stays abroad; in 1887 von Suttner met with Nobel again in Paris. She was also introduced to other Parisian notables. The topic that was of most concern in these international circles was the growing tension between France and Germany.

Von Suttner was enthusiastic about the potential of the International Arbitration and Peace Association (IAPA) and wrote what was to become her most successful and celebrated work, *Lay Down Your Arms,* in support of the IAPA and the peace movement in general. The novel recounts the trials of a woman who lives and suffers through the wars of 1859, 1864, 1866, and 1870-71. (Through these years, Austria, Prussia, France, Italy, and the German states were periodically at war with one another.) The heroine loses her husband in battle and her family in an epidemic and is exposed to numerous horrors of war. The book, which became an international best–seller, was translated into every European language, reaching its thirty-eighth edition by 1907. It shook the peace movement and was admired by Russian revolutionary Leon Trotsky, as well as Alfred Nobel.

The European peace movement. The primary goal of the European peace groups was to organize conferences aimed at encouraging agitatim for peace. Legislators exerted pressure on their governments to adopt the policies of disarmament (the abolition, reduction, or limitation of military forces and weapons) and arbitration (a process for settling disputes by submitting the issues involved to the judgment of an impartial third party, or arbitrator). The first such conference, in 1888, was sparsely attended; only French and English parliamentary representatives were present. Attendance grew in 1890, when 111 legislators took part in a meeting in London. Bertha von Suttner, who had recently moved to Vienna and become active in a newly formed Austrian Society for Friends of Peace, was encouraged to work for the success of the next peace conference, to be held in Rome. She used all of her skills to persuade influential Austrian politicians to participate.

Diplomat and journalist for peace. At the first meeting of the Austrian Society for Friends of Peace, von Suttner was elected president and nominated to serve as the Austrian representative at the Rome congress. It was a privileged position through which she gained friendships as well as international contacts.

Encouraged by the Rome congress, von Suttner cofounded *Die Waffin nieden* ("Lay Down Your Arms"), a monthly journal that soon became the voice of the peace movement. It covered international conferences and congresses, included interviews with notables in the movement, and reported on current events.

Founding an International Peace Organization

The IAPA, or International Arbitration and Peace Association, was founded in London by Hodson Pratt, a British peace activist, in 1880. His vision for the IAPA was to establish associations like the London organization throughout Britain and other European countries. The ultimate goal was to form a federation aimed at spreading a commitment to peace throughout the world.

In 1892 von Suttner was named vice-president of the International Bureau in Bern, Switzerland, a major organization that coordinated peace congresses, which at the time were operating independently of each other. The bureau also helped determine which items would be on conference agendas. It was a focal point of the peace movement, and the central headquarters for all peace societies. The lay president, as von Suttner became known, was highly respected for her diplomatic abilities. Since her work was aimed at reducing tensions among European nations and peoples, she refused to allow politics to interfere in the work of the peace movement.

Strains in the peace movement. In the years between 1892 and 1899, the European peace movement became divided into two factions: the slower-moving legislative movement, which was working to establish a permanent international court of arbitration and encouraging the formation of a European organization that would bring lasting peace; and an aggressive peace movement, which was pushing for world disarmament.

Von Suttner was interested in both courses but was severely restricted from pursuing either. She could not run for elected office because the Austrian parliament did not admit women. She was unable, therefore, to act officially as part of the conferences organized for legislators. For her and others like her, the only way of spreading the message of the peace movement was through journalism and propaganda (selected information—true or false—that is promoted with the aim of persuading people to adopt a particular belief, attitude, or course of action). So von Suttner continued to write.

By this time von Suttner had earned an international reputation as a journalist whose work was dedicated to ideas that would alleviate human suffering. Attacking what she described as the "yellow press," which aimed at whipping up public sentiment in favor of war with slander and other false information, she was dedicated to reporting what she saw as the truth.

Progress. By August 1898, von Suttner's ideas were receiving wide acceptance. The czar (or absolute ruler) of Russia issued a manifesto in which he pledged to reach out to other world leaders to form an alliance aimed at establishing peace and reducing armaments. This was seen as a major victory not only for the peace movement, but also for von Suttner; the values expressed in her writings had influenced key Russian officials. These leaders had concluded that a European war would be disastrous and agreed that a partial, limited disarmament might be wise. In an eight-point plan presented later that year, however, six of the points addressed war and only two discussed disarmament and the peaceful resolution of international disputes. Still, these events led up to a peace conference at The Hague (Netherlands) the following year.

The Hague Peace Conference. The Hague conference focused exclusively on peace and disarmament issues. In attendance were high-ranking diplomats and twenty-six other govern-

---

Alfred Nobel

Swede Alfred Bernhard Nobel (1833-1896) was the inventor of dynamite and other explosives. Around 1863 he established a factory to produce liquid nitroglycerin, a colorless, oily explosive. But when the facility blew up the following year, killing his younger brother, Nobel determined to find safe handling methods for the substance. This led to the discovery of dynamite, in which nitroglycerin is absorbed in a stable material like wood pulp. Dynamite does not explode without some sort of detonating device to set it off. Nobel also developed gelignite (gelatin dynamite).

Nobel was a lifelong pacifist, believing that peace was more important than any political objective. He wished his explosives to be used solely for peaceful purposes and was greatly embittered by their military use. He left most of his fortune for the establishment of the Nobel Foundation. This fund has been used to award Nobel prizes (awarded in peace, physics, chemistry, physiology or medicine, literature, and economics) since 1901.

ment representatives. Von Suttner was the only woman out of fifteen journalists who were allowed to cover the proceedings. (She later wrote a book on the event.) In addition to her role as a reporter, she assumed diplomatic duties, maneuvering key players through the complex political scene with the aid of her many influential contacts. An important outcome of the conference was the permanent establishment of a court of arbitration, the International Bureau at The Hague, which helps to resolve disputes in international law.

> ### More Books by Bertha von Suttner
>
> *Inventarium einer Steele* (1882)
>
> *Hanna* (1884)
>
> *Krieg und Frieden* (title translated as "War and Peace"; 1896)
>
> *Die Haagen Friedenskonferenz* ("The Hague Conference"; 1900)
>
> *Memoiren* (1909; published in English in 1910 as *Memoirs of Bertha von Suttner*)

Establishment of the Nobel Peace Prize. Von Suttner had maintained a relationship with Alfred Nobel for nearly twenty years. Throughout that time, she had attempted to gain his allegiance to the peace movement, the ultimate success of which he questioned. He had no reservations about the cause, but he at first believed that the movement, despite its many congresses and societies, would fail to achieve its ends.

Finally, von Suttner's years of correspondence and reports on the progress and promise of the movement were sufficiently convincing: in 1901 Nobel established an annual peace prize in his name, to be awarded to a man or woman who had worked to bring nations together, disband or reduce armies, or further the work of peace congresses. The first recipient of the prize was Jean Henri Dunant, the founder of the Red Cross (an international agency for the relief of victims of war or disaster). Von Suttner herself was the first female recipient of the prize when it was awarded to her in 1905.

Aftermath

Acclaimed as international peace figure. After the death of her husband in 1902, von Suttner began to pare down her public outings. Nonetheless, she continued to be admired and respected by the international community. In 1903 Prince Albert I of Monaco, who had recently established the Institut International de la Paix (International Peace Institute) aimed at recording information on war, international law, and the pacifist movement, honored her as a leading international peace figure.

Von Suttner carried on with her writing, publishing a pamphlet in 1909 entitled "Barbarity in the Skies," which advocated a prohibition against using airplanes in war. The following year, she wrote her last novel, *Man's Noblest Thought,* another critique of Austrian nobility.

Bertha von Suttner died in 1914, a few days before the start of World War I. Her legacy to the peace movement provided groundwork that led to the establishment of peace organizations such as the League of Nations (the first major international association of countries; a total of 63 states were members during the league's twenty-six-year existence) and its successor, the United Nations.

For More Information

Lengyel, Emil. *And All Her Paths Were Peace.* Nashville: Thomas Nelson, 1975.

Suttner, Bertha von. *Complete Works.* Introduction by Leopold Katscher. Vol. 1. Netherlands: Dresden, 1906.

Suttner, Bertha von. *Lay Down Your Arms.* Reprint. Staten Island, New York: Gordon Press, 1974.

The United Nations

Headquartered in New York City, the United Nations is an international organization of the world's states that aims to promote peace and international cooperation. Successor to the League of Nations, it was founded at the 1945 San Francisco Conference initiated by the "Big Three" Allied Powers of World War II (the United States, the United Kingdom, and the Soviet Union); 51 states signed the charter. Mid-1990s membership in the United Nations was more than triple that. The United Nations Security Council, one of six major organs of the organization, was intended as a permanent peacekeeping body. Peacekeeping troops are sent regularly to wartorn parts of the world. The role of these international troops can range from observation to defensive combat, the latter regularly inspiring controversy.

Emmeline Pankhurst

1858-1928

Personal Background

Early influences. Emmeline Pankhurst was born Emmeline Goulden in July 1858 in Manchester, England. She was the oldest of ten children. Mr. and Mrs. Goulden were the proprietors of a small business, and though the Goulden family owned their own land, Emmeline's parents stressed the importance of aiding the poor and disadvantaged. Mr. Goulden often offered assistance to the needy and with his wife joined the Liberal Party, the most socially concerned political party of the era. The Gouldens were also early supporters of full citizen's rights for women.

Emmeline developed an early interest in politics and the women's suffragist (or right to vote) movement. As a child she boldly wore the colors of the Liberal Party and demonstrated before polling stations in support of Liberal candidates. When Lydia Becker, a prominent suffragist and founder of the local suffrage organization, gave a passionate speech urging women and men to work together in the struggle for women's rights, she convinced the young Emmeline to become a committed suffragist.

Education and marriage. In 1872 Emmeline left England to attend a highly respected, academically oriented finishing school in Paris. (A finishing school is a private school for girls that emphasizes cultural studies and prepares students for social activities.) Upon her return, she met Dr. Richard Pankhurst, a Man-

▲ **Emmeline Pankhurst**

Event: Claiming equal rights for women.

Role: Emmeline Pankhurst was the leader of Britain's suffragette movement, the goals of which were to win British women the right to vote. With her fiery oratory and militant tactics, she forced British political leaders to act, with eventual success. Pankhurst was also a reformer in the area of public health.

chester lawyer who had been campaigning for women's rights since 1867. He had worked successfully to pass a reform bill giving women the right to vote in local elections. He was also the leader of the local peace party. Though he was twenty years her senior, Emmeline married Pankhurst in 1878.

Early politics in Manchester and London. Emmeline became involved in the Manchester suffrage society in 1878. She was convinced that direct influence on the government was the surest path to women's rights. To that end, she encouraged her husband to run for a seat in the British Parliament. He waged an unsuccessful campaign on the Independent Liberal and the Liberal tickets. It was the first of many attempts he would make to be elected to office.

The Pankhursts, who by this time had three daughters, Christabel, Sylvia, and Adela, and a son, Frank, moved to London in 1880. Aided by her sister Mary, Emmeline opened a small shop; she was determined to prove that women could run a business and, therefore, were surely capable of handling the vote. Unfortunately, the location of the shop and lack of interest in the goods sold there made the business a short-lived venture.

Later that year, tragedy struck the Pankhurst household: Frank became ill with diphtheria and died. In her grief, Emmeline resolved to fight for better health and living conditions for the poor.

Working with Manchester's poor. Moving back to Manchester in 1894, Emmeline became a member of the Women's Franchise League. (Franchise here refers to the right to vote.) She established a relief committee to aid the poor, and later, a subcommittee that concentrated specifically on the care of women and children.

Having proven her capabilities on the committees of the Women's Franchise League, Emmeline was elected to the Board of Poor Law Guardians, a government committee that oversaw the

---

Dr. Richard Pankhurst

Emmeline's considerably older husband, Dr. Richard Pankhurst, was an acquaintance of the great British philosopher, economist, and social worker John Stuart Mill. Midway into the nineteenth century, Mill had organized the first society for women's rights and had written a much discussed article on the "Admission of Women to the Electoral Franchise." Richard Pankhurst had joined that first women's rights group long before Emmeline began her efforts.

▲ Pankhurst speaking at a rally for women's suffrage on Wall Street in New York City, circa 1911. After a huge rally in London's Hyde Park, Pankhurst was arrested and jailed for three months.

use of tax revenue set aside for the poor. The committee was responsible for constructing workhouses, where the destitute were housed and assigned work in order to earn room and board. Emmeline's first concern was the quality of food served to workhouse residents, and she led the way in reforming workhouse menus. This reform was followed by others, including the replacement of worn or broken furniture and the construction of a new school. The experience convinced Emmeline that it was possible to improve the life of the working class.

Insights into the lives of Britain's women. Richard Pankhurst died suddenly later in 1894, leaving Emmeline alone and responsible for the welfare of three children. Through her connections on the Board of Poor Law Guardians, she obtained a position as registrar of births and deaths, a job that brought her into the homes and lives of Manchester's poorest women. She met women who had been deserted by their husbands or boyfriends and were struggling to support themselves and their children with no financial assistance.

Pankhurst also served on the Manchester School Board, a position that allowed her a view of the labor issues facing women. Women teachers, for example, were paid less than men of equal training and experience. In addition to their standard courses, women were forced to teach subjects such as sewing and home economics without pay. In general, women were barred from attending professional schools and denied skilled jobs because of men's fears of wage competition. Pankhurst added these concerns to her agenda for women's rights.

A new partner. In 1903 Pankhurst's eldest daughter, Christabel, who had been sent to Switzerland to study, returned home. She had planned to obtain a doctor of law degree but had been barred, as had other British women, from seeking an advanced degree. She decided to study for a bachelor's degree instead. Christabel had exhibited an early interest in women's suffrage, and upon obtaining her degree, she joined her mother in the campaign, becoming an inseparable partner and ally.

Participation:
Claiming Equal Rights for Women

Founding WSPU. Existing women's suffrage groups had proven ineffective, so Pankhurst and Christabel, along with a small group of women supporters, founded the Women's Social and Political Union (WSPU) in 1903. Then, in order to promote the fledgling, unknown group, the Pankhursts toured the North of England, promoting WSPU and women's suffrage on lecture tours and at traveling fairs. Their efforts spread the WSPU to Yorkshire and Lancaster.

Pankhurst and the WSPU then focused their attention on Parliament. They successfully enlisted a member of Parliament,

Keir Hardie, the Independent Labour leader, to sponsor a women's suffrage bill, but the members of Parliament deliberately stalled actions on the floor of the House of Commons until time to debate the issue had run out. This was a clear indication of law-makers' unwillingness to even consider women's suffrage as a worthy legislative issue.

This inspired Pankhurst and her followers to attend the forums of political parties and challenge the politicians present to act on behalf of women's suffrage. They hoped direct confronta-tion would force candidates and elected officials to address the issue. Such challenging of authority was a bold move for women at that time, and many paid a price for their defiance.

Christabel and Annie Kenney, a factory worker who was to become a champion of the suffrage movement, attempted to ques-tion politicians at a Liberal Party forum in Manchester. They were roughly removed from the hall and arrested after raising their voices to ask questions and then unfurling a "Votes for Women" banner. Theirs were the first in a long line of arrests, and their imprisonment brought much-needed attention to the suffrage cause. The press, however, was critical of these radical women; a national newspaper coined the term "suffragette" (the diminutive of "suffragist," as the older women in the movement were called) to label these new activists.

Building WSPU. In order to take on Parliament directly, WSPU moved its headquarters from Manchester to London in 1906. There, the organization was funded by a wealthy London couple, the Penthick-Lawrences. Mrs. Penthick-Lawrence was made honorary WSPU treasurer, and the couple edited the Union's new newspaper, *Votes for Women*. Pankhurst steered the activism of WSPU in an entirely different course from that of the older, more established groups. Radicalism—arrests and protests—continued to generate publicity for the cause and demonstrated women's determination to win equality, whatever the consequences.

As a result of WSPU's new visibility, Pankhurst was invited to be part of a delegation of representatives of established women's organizations who were attempting to address Britain's prime

▲ Pankhurst being arrested outside of Buckingham Palace in London
while trying to present a petition to King George V on May 21, 1914.

minister on women's issues. The prime minister refused to consider their ideas, and Pankhurst concluded that radical means,
not diplomacy, were the only way to raise the consciousness of a
deaf government.

Women's Parliament. In light of the continuing refusal of Parliament to even acknowledge the idea of women's suffrage, Pankhurst convened a Women's Parliament in 1907. A referendum was passed by the attendees that demanded women's suffrage be discussed in Parliament. Still, the House of Commons refused to consider the issue.

Militancy. Parliamentary obstinance inspired Pankhurst to call for an increase in militant (more aggressive) activism. WSPU members continued to hold protest rallies at various houses of government. The number of arrests increased, but no political or legislative success was forthcoming. After a huge rally in London's Hyde Park, attended by over a million women, Pankhurst was arrested and jailed for six months for "inciting an uprising." Her sentence was reduced to three months after her passionate speech on the ethics of women's suffrage moved the presiding judge.

> ### The First Violence
>
> On February 13, 1908, Pankhurst led a band of thirteen women who stormed the House of Commons. The action so stirred women's groups that three days of riots in London followed. For inciting the riots, Pankhurst spent six weeks in jail—the first of many prison terms she received in service to women's rights.

Immediately Pankhurst introduced new tactics, including urging women to break windows and to chain themselves to House of Commons grills in the "Ladies' Gallery." The arrests continued, climaxing with "Black Friday," when a group of women who had protested being denied a meeting with the prime minister were brutally beaten by police and male bystanders.

The campaign took on an entirely new dimension when the suffragettes demanded "political prisoner" status and began to use hunger strikes as a political tool. Forced feedings were instituted at many prisons, and the emaciated, ill-looking women emerging from the jails became public martyrs, drawing increased sympathy from the British people.

More extreme measures. As the campaign continued, the membership of WSPU began to change. A group of union supporters who challenged Pankhurst's leadership broke off and formed a new organization called the Women's Freedom League. But WSPU membership also broadened as influential musicians, painters, and dancers, as well as the wives and daughters of prominent politicians and wealthy men joined Pankhurst's organization.

The group's militancy, which increased in 1910 and 1911, began to include raids on government houses and offices, arson, destruction of telephone lines and private property, and even the bombing of the residence of the home secretary. The latter action cost Pankhurst and the WSPU the patronage of the Penthick-Lawrences. More alarming, Pankhurst was sentenced to three years of hard labor for the deed, the first time a woman had been so harshly sentenced.

World War I turns the tide. By 1914 government opposition began to crumble. World War I advanced the women's cause in the workplace and on the political front. Pankhurst was asked by the prime minister to organize a rally calling for women to replace men in ammunition factories. She was also chosen as a representative of Britain in Russia following the overthrow of the czar's regime there; the Russians had withdrawn from the Allied pact (a union of nations battling Germany in the war), and Britain wanted them to rejoin. Although Pankhurst was unsuccessful in convincing Russia to rejoin the war effort, she did succeed in persuading women to fill many wartime jobs in Britain.

The women wartime workers attracted positive press and gained even more public support. Their service finally convinced the government; in 1917, shortly before the end of the war, a limited franchise gave women over the age of thirty the right to vote. In 1918 the bill became law, and a second bill was introduced giving women the right to run for Parliament. After years of struggle, Pankhurst had finally realized her dream.

Aftermath

Public health activist. After winning women's rights to vote and hold office, Pankhurst continued her activism in the field of public health. In 1919 she was nominated chief lecturer on public health, and in 1921 she joined the National Council for Combating Venereal Diseases, launching an educational campaign throughout Canada and attracting large audiences because of her suffragist fame. In 1928 she was a candidate for the House of Commons on the Conservative ticket. She was defeated, but soon saw a law enacted that extended the franchise to all women over twenty-one years of age. Pankhurst died later that year.

Activist daughters. Pankhurst's daughters continued their work for women's rights. Christabel had been one of the leaders of the WSPU alongside her mother, and Sylvia and Adela had worked for the cause internationally. The latter two had socialist leanings—Sylvia had campaigned to make socialists of workers in London's East End, though she was best known for her 1940s campaign to win the vote for women in the northeast African nation of Ethiopia. (Socialism is an economic philosophy and political movement that aims to achieve a just, classless society through public ownership and operation of the means of production and distribution of goods.) Adela became the leader of the socialist/feminist movement for women's emancipation in Australia.

For More Information

Foster, G. Allen. *Votes for Women.* New York: Criterion Books, 1966.

Kraditor, Aileen W. *The Ideas of the Woman Suffrage Movement 1890-1920.* New York: Columbia University Press, 1965.

Mitchell, David J. *The Fighting Pankhursts: A Study in Tenacity.* New York: Macmillan, 1967.

Noble, Iris. *Emmeline and Her Daughters: The Pankhurst Suffragettes.* New York: J. Messner, 1971.

Pankhurst, Emmeline. *My Own Story.* 1904. Reprint. Westport, Connecticut: Greenwood Press, 1985.

Rosa Luxemburg

1870-1919

Personal Background

Warsaw and Jewish identity. Rosa Luxemburg (whose name was originally Rozalia Luksenburg) was born in Zamosc, Poland, in 1870, the youngest of five children. As Polish Jews living in the time of pogroms—officially condoned mob attacks on Jewish communities—Rosa's parents rejected their Jewish cultural heritage, even moving to Warsaw to further the assimilation into Euro-Christian society. Thus, as Rosa grew older, she identified strongly with Polish, rather than Jewish, traditions. In fact, her hatred of her Jewish heritage developed into strong anti-Semitism.

Early influences. Somehow the family managed to enroll Rosa in one of the finest girls' high schools in Warsaw. She did well there, qualifying for a gold medal (though it was denied her because of her rebellious antics). Before she graduated at age seventeen, however, Rosa was already caught up in socialist ideas.

During her teenage years, Rosa was influenced by the verse of a Polish poet named Adam Mickiewicz. He envisioned a social order based on equality, which he predicted would replace the old distinctions between rich and poor. Community, he argued, must be bound by one noble goal, and that was freedom for all people—not only the people of Poland but of all nations oppressed by their own or foreign governments. Mickiewicz believed that everyone

▲ Rosa Luxemburg

Event: Attempting socialist revolution.

Role: Rosa Luxemburg helped shape the turbulent Marxist and socialist movements in Europe at the turn of the twentieth century. Particularly effective in Russia, Poland, and Germany, she was a revolutionary leader from the late nineteenth century through the end of World War I.

had a moral obligation to effect social change. As soon as she graduated from high school, Rosa joined a socialist group in Russia, the Proletariat.

Rosa was also influenced by several strong, intellectual Polish women revolutionaries who were involved in active struggles for the emancipation of the working class. Aleksandra Jentys was one of the most prominent; she was at the forefront of the Polish workers movement in the 1880s.

Russian occupation. The tense social and political situation in Poland during Rosa's youth had encouraged challenges to the old order. Russia had occupied parts of Poland for a century. Land reform had once allowed for land to be redistributed to the peasants. But later it became illegal for Poles to own any land at all.

Meanwhile, Russia was trying to bring itself and Poland into the industrial age. Polish workers had no control over this struggle. The workers fell deeper and deeper into poverty and from time to time protested their lot, only to be beaten by their Russian overlords. Still, literature from the West (Western Europe) was studied in secret.

Two forces were shaping radical ideas in the occupied nation: a movement called *Narodnaja Voeja,* or the People's Will, which called for instant political action, including terror tactics, to achieve revolution; and Marxism, which claimed that only an educated working class could achieve revolution and which rejected the use of terror in that effort. (After the 1905 violence in Russia, Luxemburg would abandon her pacifist teachings.)

Luxemburg became a firm Marxist and a champion of socialism in Russian-occupied Poland. By the age of nineteen, she had become so active in the Polish socialist movement that the Russian government in Poland had targeted her for arrest. The choice for Luxemburg was imprisonment, possibly in the remote Russian region of Siberia, or exile. She chose exile to Zurich, Switzerland. Zurich was a hotbed of socialist activity; the city also offered her the opportunity to attend college—a privilege denied women in Russian lands.

Early politics: From Poland to Switzerland. In 1890 Luxemburg enrolled at the University of Zurich. Switzerland appeared incredibly civilized and tolerant, a promised land after the repression of Warsaw. At the university, Luxemburg met a Berlin socialist and writer, Karl Lubeck, who had been expelled from Germany by its antisocialist government. He introduced her to the political press. Luxemburg eagerly followed his lead and started to write and edit political articles. It was the beginning of a long career in political journalism.

A few months after Luxemburg arrived in Zurich, she met Leo Jogiches, a man with whom she was to have an intense political collaboration and longtime love affair. He had been born in Lithuania to a wealthy, privileged family but had used his money to fight for the workers' revolution there. At twenty-three, Jogiches was already a well-known, respected political agitator in the workers' movement. He had formed the Jewish Workers Union and the Wilmo Central Organization. Jogiches took an immediate interest in Rosa. In her, he saw a future orator and leader who would further the aims of socialism.

A Marxist political party based in Poland. In 1892 Luxemburg proposed the idea of creating a Marxist political party based in Poland. The following year, Luxemburg and Jogiches formed the Social Democracy for the Kingdom of Poland Party (SDKP) and established a socialist newspaper, *Sprawa Robotwicza* ("Worker's Cause"); the press, they felt, would be an important educational and propaganda tool. (Propaganda is selected information—true or false—that is promoted with the aim of persuading people to adopt a particular belief, attitude, or course of action).

Beginnings of the SDKP. From the beginning, Luxemburg was the chief spokesperson and a key strategist of the SDKP. She began to campaign for the recognition of the organization at the Second International Congress of the socialist movement, held in Zurich. Though the party was unsuccessful at the Zurich conference, it was recognized at the 1896 London conference.

From 1893 to 1900, Luxemburg put all of her energies into expanding the power and influence of the SDKP and finishing her doctorate at the university. She worked on the party newspaper, wrote speeches, and formed alliances with other similarly oriented groups. By 1897, with a published doctoral thesis and over fifty articles to her credit, the foundation had been laid for a successful move to Germany, which also occupied Polish land, in order to expand the base of the SDKP.

The Marriage of Rosa Luxemburg

In 1898 Rosa Luxemburg married a German citizen, Gustav Lubeck. The marriage was arranged by Lubeck's mother. For Luxemburg, the union was merely a convenience—a way for her to become active in the German socialist movement. According to one account, "After the ceremony, the bride and groom shook hands on the steps of the registry office and parted company. They would never live together, and would only rarely, by chance, see one another (Florence, p. 80)."

Upon her arrival in Germany, Luxemburg immediately became active in SDKP politics. Her first assignment was to agitate Polish workers in German-occupied Upper Silesia and win their support for SDKP candidates in the upcoming election. She met with resounding success.

A leader in the socialist movement. In less than ten years, Luxemburg had established herself as a leader in the Polish and German social democratic parties. By 1901 she was a respected expert on Eastern European affairs. Believing that the pen was capable of calling people to action and bringing about revolution, she wrote frequently about subjects important to the socialist movement, including universal voting rights in Eastern Europe, arms, freedom of artistic expression, and the works of Marx and Mickiewicz. In 1902 she founded the newspaper *Gazeta Ludova* ("Worker's Gazette"). But the newspaper, which was aimed at uniting German and Polish workers, was largely ineffective.

Luxemburg began to expand her influence internationally when, in 1903, she became a member of the International Socialist Bureau. In the International Congress held that year in Amsterdam, the Netherlands, she represented Poland and Germany. She was the only woman present among the prominent international socialist leaders. The goals of the movement were based on Luxemburg's famous critical work "Social Reform or Revolution."

Bloody Sunday and its aftermath. When peacefully striking Russian workers were fired upon by government troops in what was later known as the "Bloody Sunday" massacre of 1905, sparking strikes throughout Poland and Russia, Luxemburg recognized the potential for revolution and stepped up her editorial and political work. Russian-annexed Poland erupted as Poles protested the Russification of their land and culture. As students, sailors, peasants, and intellectuals joined strikers throughout the occupied lands, martial (or military enforced) law was ordered. Russia claimed it would introduce a Polish constitution and increase civil liberties, but these proved to be empty promises.

In 1906 Luxemburg was imprisoned in Russia for possessing illegal SDKP materials; she continued to conduct business from jail. When she returned to Germany, she pressed the SDKP leadership to call for a Marxist revolution, but in the end, they were unwilling to commit to revolution beyond theorizing.

Critiqued own socialism. In a series of articles and speeches written from 1904 to 1908, Luxemburg reviewed her own ideas on socialism, which were much like those of Marx. Marxism, she argued, was a humanistic philosophy (one centered on basic human values) that called for restoring wholeness to people. The goal of revolution was to fight for a more humane system. Furthermore, socialism could only be demanded by the people, not a central party authority.

Luxemburg continued to try to persuade the leadership of the German Social Democrat Party (SPD) to yield power to the workers and help them in their attempts to end their political and economic oppression. In 1913, even with the threat of a European war growing, she criticized the German SPD for supporting a government property tax earmarked for military expenditures. This, she felt, was further oppression of the workers.

In Defense of Marxism

Luxemburg displayed her intellectual aptitude with her critique of the writings of Eduard Bernstein, who argued that Marx was wrong when he theorized that class struggle would eventually lead to revolution. Luxemburg responded with "Social Reform or Revolution," a rebuttal that was praised by socialists as comprehensive and scholarly. She became an instant celebrity on the international socialist scene and was named editor-in-chief of the prestigious journal *Sachsiche Arbeiterzeitung,* the first and only woman to be accorded that honor.

▲ Believing that the pen was capable of calling people to action and bringing about revolution, Luxemburg wrote frequently about subjects important to the socialist movement.

World War I. Luxemburg spent 1915 to 1918 in prison, having been convicted of public disobedience. While in prison, she wrote several essays discussing war and its effects on the socialist movement. In "The Crisis of Social Democracy," also known as the "Junius Pamphlet," she accused the SPD of joining the war-inspired move toward breaking international socialism into national units. In the "Spartacus Letters," she decried World War I as a defeat of socialism and democracy and a return to barbarism.

Spartacist uprising in Germany. In November 1918, there began a short-lived uprising in Germany called the Spartacist Movement, which attempted to effect socialist revolution by capitalizing on political confusion following the end of the war. Wilhelm II had given up control of Germany and starvation was widespread throughout the country. Luxemburg, who had just been released from prison, started a Spartacus League newspaper in support of the uprising, titled *The Red Flag*. Two months later, government troops overwhelmed the activists, ending the brief rebellion.

Aftermath

Targeted by government. Luxemburg continued to support socialist revolution in her writings. With Spartacist leader Karl Liebknecht, she helped form the German Communist Party out of the core of the Spartacist League. An attempt by the party to seize power in 1919 was crushed by the German government, and Liebknecht and Luxemburg were murdered while under arrest.

A ban was placed on Luxemburg's works for several decades at the insistence of Russian communist dictator Josef Stalin. Only in the past few decades have her works and her life been publicly examined.

Who Were the Spartacists?

In the desperate situation in Germany after World War I, several socialist factions took the opportunity to stir up riots with the eventual aim of effecting revolution. The most extreme group was led by Karl Liebknecht, who wrote under the disguised name of Spartacus (the leader of a slave revolt in ancient Rome). Liebknecht, who was eventually joined by Luxemburg in his agitations to violence, started several riots in and around Berlin that resulted in the deaths of thousands of protesters.

For More Information

Abraham, Richard. *Luxemburg: A Life for the International.* New York: St. Martin's, 1989.

Ettinger, Elzbieta. *Luxemburg: A Life.* Oxford, England: Berb, 1986.

Florence, Ronald. *Marx's Daughters: Eleanor Marx, Rosa Luxemburg, Angelica Balbanoff.* New York: Dial, 1975.

Frölich, Paul. *Rosa Luxemburg, Her Life and Work.* London: Left Book, 1940.

Science Exploring the Unseen World

1873

William Clerk Maxwell publishes his equations unifying electricity and magnetism.

1895

Sigmund Freud publishes *Studies in Hysteria* (with Joseph Breuer), considered the founding work of psychoanalysis.

1897

Marie Curie begins investigating radioactivity.

1898

Curie isolates polonium and radium.

1900

Max Planck introduces the idea of the quantum. Freud publishes *The Interpretation of Dreams*, considered his most important work.

1905

Albert Einstein publishes revolutionary works in physics, including the special theory of relativity.

1911

Ernest Rutherford announces his discoveries about atomic structure.

1916

Einstein publishes the general theory of relativity.

1923

Edwin Hubble identifies galaxies beyond the Milky Way.

1929

Hubble describes an expanding universe.

1936

Hubble publishes *The Realm of the Nebulae*.

SCIENCE EXPLORING THE UNSEEN WORLD

At the end of the nineteenth century, the sciences were primed for revolutionary changes in both the kinds of questions scientists sought to answer and how they asked them. In the past, men and women of science had concerned themselves primarily with everyday experience. Sir Isaac Newton's laws of motion, for example, could be explained in terms of common objects like the movement of billiard balls or apples falling to the ground. Basic mathematics and simple equipment like magnets or microscopes were the tools of the day. By the early twentieth century, however, science had entered a whole new world, a realm far beyond the daily experiences of most researchers.

Nowhere was this more true than in the rapidly changing science of physics. Groundwork for breakthroughs in this field was laid by Michael Faraday and James Clerk Maxwell, British scientists who established that electricity and magnetism were in fact a single force, electromagnetism. By the 1870s, Maxwell had explained this discovery with mathematical equations. Describing in detail how electromagnetic waves (including light) move through space and time, Maxwell's equations pushed physics ahead in terms of what they could explain—and what they could not.

In 1895 German physicist Wilhelm Roentgen discovered X-rays, which soon proved to be a form of electromagnetic radiation of a much higher energy level than visible light. The following year, a French scientist named Henri Becquerel happened upon what seemed to be a similar sort of radiation. When Polish-born physicist **Marie Curie** began investigating Becquerel's radiation, she realized that it emanated from the atoms of the substances in which it was found. She described these substances as "radioactive." Curie worked closely with the materials to isolate, or separate out, the radioactive elements present within them. For her groundbreaking work in atomic radiation, Curie won two Nobel Prizes, in 1903 and 1911.

Curie's pioneering efforts led to a greater understanding of the atom. In 1911 British physicist Ernest Rutherford announced his discovery that the atom contains a central nucleus around which one or more particles (called electrons) travel in an orbit. Rutherford's work inspired a greater search for an accurate description of atomic particles and their behavior. Physicists had previously made some progress in solving the puzzle. In 1900, for example, German physicist Max Planck had suggested that energy is made up of tiny units, called quanta.

Then came **Albert Einstein.** In 1905 Einstein published three scientific papers of great originality and importance. In the first, he applied Planck's idea of quanta to light, boldly ignoring Maxwell's pronouncement that light is made of waves and suggesting instead that it is made up of distinct units, quanta of light (later called photons). In the second paper, he definitively proved the existence of atoms. And in the third, he introduced his "special theory" of relativity, which equaled Planck's notions about quanta in its outrageous violation of accepted ideas. Einstein's theory held that observations of space, time, and matter were relative to the position of the observer.

These two ideas—relativity and quanta—took physics into uncharted territory. Light, according to quantum physics, can behave either as a wave or as a particle, depending on how we decide to measure it. If we measure it as a wave, it appears to stop behaving like a particle; if we measure it as a particle, it appears to stop behaving like a wave.

Relativity influenced virtually every scientific field. In astronomy, relativity contributed to new ways of measuring the building blocks of the universe, and even to the reexamination of ideas about how the universe was created. **Edwin Hubble** built on the work of astronomer Henrietta Leavitt to discover galaxies beyond our own Milky Way; he then used what was known about relativity to measure the distance of galaxies from Earth and to study their behavior. Hubble's observations changed our conception of the universe, expanding our interests farther into space—the cosmos—thus creating a new science, cosmology, the study of the universe in its entirety.

The human mind. Also during this period, science was making strides in yet another area, one equally strange and mysterious: the human mind. The science of psychology had developed slowly over the course of the nineteenth century. The work of **Sigmund Freud,** however, was in its own way as revolutionary as Einstein's, and perhaps equally influential.

Freud's practice of medicine revealed that some illnesses originate in the mind, not the body. Freud called his theories and the "talking cure" he pioneered to help treat them "psychoanalysis." He believed that by discussing painful memories, experiences that his patients had "repressed," or kept hidden deep within themselves, patients could relieve physical symptoms of illness.

Freud was among the first to recognize a series of simultaneous emotional growth stages that children go through as they grow. He made clear how these stages determine the character of the adult who grows out of the child. Freud developed the concept of "sibling rivalry"—where sisters and brothers become rivals for the attention of parents—an idea that is now taken for granted. Among his other major theories was that of the Oedipus complex. This theory holds that at some point in childhood, a child develops a romantic attraction to the parent of the opposite sex and an adversarial relationship with the parent of the same sex.

Though not all of Freud's ideas are accepted by modern psychologists and psychiatrists, many of his basic discoveries have proven to be key in understanding human behavior and personality. Freud took steps toward examining our inner selves, a depth as new to inquiry and as mysterious as Hubble's cosmos.

Albert Einstein

1879-1955

Personal Background

Albert Einstein was born in the German town of Ulm on March 14, 1879. Soon afterwards, his parents, Hermann and Pauline Einstein, moved to Munich, one of Germany's largest cities. Albert and his sister, Maja, who was two and a half years his junior, were raised and educated there. Though his family was Jewish, they were not very religious, and Albert attended a Catholic school as a boy.

Compass. Einstein hated the stiff, military discipline of the German school system. He had his own way of learning. Once, when he was about four or five and sick in bed, his father gave him a compass to play with. Einstein would always remember the wonder that gripped him when he saw the compass needle move. He felt driven to understand what strange force kept it pointing north no matter how he turned it. This curiosity would always be his own compass, keeping him pointed firmly in a single direction: the direction of understanding.

"Holy geometry book." From a very early age, an intense desire to understand the forces that govern the physical world drew Einstein to mathematics and science. Largely ignoring his classes, he studied and read on his own, far above the level of his classmates. When he was twelve, his Uncle Jakob gave him a book on geometry by the ancient Greek mathematician Euclid.

▲ **Albert Einstein**

Event: Formulating the theory of relativity.

Role: Albert Einstein, "the last classical physicist," developed a theory of relativity that destroyed forever the basic assumption that ideas like motion and time had definite, "absolute" values. Einstein's theory held that observations of movement and time depend completely on who is doing the observing. In other words, events are "relative" to the movement and place in time of the observer and have no independent, absolute value.

The simplicity and power of Euclid's geometry hit him with the force of a religious revelation—indeed, he called it "the holy geometry book" (Hoffman, p. 23).

As a young boy, Einstein had gone through a religious phase, but his growing knowledge of science made him unwilling to believe what he read in the scriptures. His reluctance to accept religious authority was part of a larger suspicion of any kind of authority. What Einstein loved about science and mathematics was that you never had to take someone else's word, but could always test ideas with your own experiments or calculations. Later, Einstein would say, "To punish me for my contempt for authority, Fate made me an authority myself" (Hoffman, p. 24).

Switzerland. At fifteen Einstein was doing so poorly in school that he decided to drop out for a year and go to Italy, where his parents were living for a short time. It was a carefree period during which he saw the sights, spent time with his family, and went hiking with friends. Then, without having earned his high school diploma, he took the exam for the Zurich (Switzerland) Polytechnic Institute, where he hoped to study engineering. He failed the exam, but one of the professors there advised him to try again after another year of high school. The professor recommended he attend the Swiss Cantonal (state) School at Aargau in the meantime.

Slow as a Child

During his childhood, Einstein was thought to be rather slow. For example, he didn't begin talking until he was about three, much later than other children. Later, one of his teachers told him, "You will never amount to anything" (Hoffman, p. 20).

There, for once, Einstein found a school where ideas about teaching were not based on military discipline and memorization. Instead, he was able to learn the way he liked, by asking questions and working on a problem until he had an answer.

In 1896 Einstein entered the Zurich Polytechnic, where his habit of skipping classes and studying on his own came close to getting him in trouble. Luckily, his friend Marcel Grossman went to every lecture and took excellent notes, which he shared with Einstein. Grossman's notes probably saved Einstein from failing. On his own, Einstein was struggling with new ideas in physics that his teachers were not addressing. (Physics is a science that explores the physical properties and composition of objects and

▲ Einstein and his first wife, Mileva Maric; married in 1903, the couple divorced amicably in 1919.

the forces that effect them.) The classes all seemed so useless. For his final exams, Einstein had to cram so hard that he thought he'd never want to think about science again.

Participation:
Formulating the Theory of Relativity

Patent Office. After graduating in 1900, Einstein, looking for a teaching job, faced two years of refusal and rejection. None of his teachers gave him a recommendation; he had bothered them too much with his endless questions and refusal to believe their answers. Finally, he found a job at the Patent Office in Bern, Switzerland. The job required engineering knowledge that he did not have, but Grossman's father knew the office's director and got Einstein an interview. Something impressed the director, perhaps Einstein's knowledge of physics. He gave Einstein a job in 1902, and for the next few years Einstein worked full time at the Patent Office.

In 1903 Einstein married a young woman, Mileva Maric, whom he had known in Zurich. (The couple would have two sons, Hans Albert, born in 1904, and Eduard, born in 1910, before divorcing amicably in 1919.) In his spare time Einstein pressed forward in physics. He was now pursuing avenues of exploration where few had gone before.

***Annalen der Physik,* 1905.** Even before beginning his job at the Patent Office, Einstein had published several scientific papers in the leading journal *Annalen der Physik* (Annals of Physics). He continued to have papers published over the next few years. In 1905 the journal printed five of his papers. The first won him his doctoral degree from the University of Zurich.

The next three papers, published together as volume 17 of the *Annalen,* make that volume a collector's item today; those libraries lucky enough to possess a copy keep them under lock and key. Each of the three papers was a short masterpiece. In the first, Einstein offered the first mathematical proof that atoms exist. (Atoms are the tiny particles of which all things are composed.) In the second, he challenged the accepted ideas of the day in suggesting that light is made up of particles. (Most scientists thought light was made of waves). And in the third, usually called the "special theory of relativity," Einstein destroyed science's previously held ideas about space and time.

Special relativity. The year 1905 would have made Einstein one of the century's leading physicists even if he had not conceived of relativity. That discovery, however, put him in a league of his own. "Special" relativity has two main ideas, ideas that are simple in themselves but can produce complicated consequences. The first is that measurements of time, space, and motion are relative.

To illustrate the idea of relativity, pretend that you have just fired a gun. The bullet goes speeding off into the distance at, say, 500 miles per hour. Imagine also that an airplane has swooped down just as you fired the gun, and it, too, is going 500 miles per hour in the same direction. The pilot ends up flying along right next to the bullet. To him, the bullet looks like it is standing still.

And it is—*relative to him.* Einstein believed that perceptions of time and space were also relative to the person perceiving them.

The second key idea behind special relativity is that the first idea has one very big exception—the one non-relative element in any situation is the speed of light. According to Einstein, the speed of light is constant (approximately 186,281 miles per second; a light-year measures the distance light travels in a year, roughly 5,878,000,000,000 miles). Thus the speed of light is the same no matter who is measuring that speed.

The formula Einstein used to express his special theory of relativity was $E=mc^2$ ("E" stands for energy—in this formula, the ability to perform work; "m" stands for mass—the amount of matter, or material substance, in an object; and "c" stands for the constant velocity [speed] of light). This formula expresses in mathematical terms that energy is actually equivalent to mass, and that changes in mass, dimension (which determines an object's position in space), and time result from increased velocity.

Gravity. Einstein's 1905 papers took some time to be fully understood by other scientists. In the meantime, he refined his various theories and continued his work at the Patent Office. His goal now was to apply his ideas about relativity to one of the biggest questions in physics: the nature of gravity. Using calculus (a branch of mathematics dealing with continuously varying quantities), Isaac Newton had described gravitational effects in the early 1600s, but that wasn't the same as defining exactly what gravitation is. "Compared with this problem," Einstein wrote to a friend, "the original theory of relativity is child's play" (Hoffman, p. 116).

Pacifism. As he worked toward finding a definition of gravity, Einstein grew more and more respected in the scientific world. Beginning in 1909, he won several teaching jobs, each one

If a Train Were Traveling at the Speed of Light....

One of the questions Einstein asked himself while in school at Aargau was: what would happen if a train was traveling at the speed of light and the engineer turned on the headlights? It took Einstein a decade to find the answer, which was that nothing would happen (because in order for the headlights to shine—or rather, for our eyes to perceive the light shining from them—the light coming out of the lamps would have to move even faster than the train). The theory of relativity, in part, was Einstein's answer to that question.

better than the last. He taught in Zurich, at the Polytechnic and at the University of Zurich, and in Prague (then in Czechoslovakia, now the Czech Republic). In 1913 he was offered the director's post at the new Kaiser Wilhelm Institute for Physics in Berlin, Germany. There, with only light teaching duties, he could focus on his research.

In 1914 World War I broke out. German scientists generally supported the war, and many of them signed a "Manifesto to the Civilized World" that defended the German military buildup. Before accepting his job in Berlin, Einstein had reflected on his hatred of that same militarism in German society when he was a child. He now supported a friend of his who wrote a "Manifesto to the Europeans" opposing German aggression and the war and calling for international peace. Einstein was one of only four who dared sign it. Later, Einstein would call for a single world government. He had become a pacifist, a person who values peace above all political concerns. He believed, too, that scientists had no business fighting wars.

General relativity. In 1916 Einstein finally finished his long and difficult work on "general" relativity. This theory is enormously complex and was much harder for other scientists to fully understand than had been special relativity. In fact, by the 1920s, special relativity was helping scientists in their daily work on subjects like the atom and quantum physics. By contrast, general relativity, while seen to be important, was less useful in daily research. Only in the 1960s, when cosmology (the study of the universe as a whole) became more popular, did general relativity become as useful a daily tool for scientists. Still, Einstein's theory

More Triumphs of 1905

Brownian Motion. Einstein's second paper of 1905 (the first was his doctoral thesis) explained the movement observed in tiny particles, such as pollen, that float in liquids. Called Brownian motion after the man who discovered it, the movement could be explained, Einstein suggested, by repeated impact on the particles by randomly moving atoms and molecules (particles made of atoms) in the liquid. His theory was later proved correct.

Light Quanta (Photons). In his second major paper of 1905, Einstein explained the "photoelectric effect," in which light striking certain metals makes them give off electrons (negatively charged particles that orbit the nucleus [core] of an atom). Einstein suggested that in order to knock the electrons away, light had to be something you could think of as a particle, a "piece" of light (later called a photon). Such tiny pieces of energy or matter are called "quanta." Einstein's idea helped create the new science of quantum physics, which studies quanta.

▲ A young Einstein in his studio in Berlin in the early 1920s; though less useful to daily research in the 1920s, Einstein's theory of general relativity turned him into a celebrity almost overnight.

of general relativity turned him into a celebrity almost overnight, earning him a fame unmatched by any other living scientist.

General relativity's main idea is that gravity is not so much a *force* as it is *geometry*—the geometry of space. Big objects like planets bend the space around them; smaller objects simply follow the bending of space. Since the special theory of relativity incorporates not just matter but also time, when scientists discuss relativity, they refer not just to space—they think instead in terms of *space-time,* in which space and time together can be affected by matter. Matter bends the fabric of space-time.

Einstein's fame skyrocketed in 1919 when British astronomers proved his general theory of relativity during a solar eclipse, confirming his prediction that the Sun's gravity bends the light from distant stars when that light passes near the Sun. Or rather, the Sun's gravity bends the space around the light from distant stars; the light actually moves along a straight path, but through bent space.

Aftermath

Princeton. Since Einstein was a Jew, his popularity in Germany was tainted by suspicion. Germany in the 1920s and 1930s was blighted by widespread anti-Semitism. Jews were blamed for many problems, including the defeat of Germany in World War I and the severe economic depression that gripped the country afterward. Einstein and his second wife, Elsa (distant cousins and childhood playmates, the two married in 1919), often visited the United States. They were on one such trip in 1933 when Adolf Hitler came to power. They realized that they could never return to Germany. (Institutionalized anti-Semitism would reach a peak during World War II when six million Jews, as well as countless members of other groups who did not fit Hitler's idea of "Aryan" perfection, would be systematically killed in concentrations camps, a genocide called the Holocaust.) Einstein accepted a position at the new Institute for Advanced Study in the small college town of Princeton, New Jersey.

What Is Matter?

Virtually everything in the universe is made up of matter, which is simply defined as "material substance." Matter is anything that has weight or fills space. Physical matter can take the forms of solid, liquid, or gas. But matter may also be considered as a specialized form of energy.

During World War II, Einstein temporarily abandoned his practice of pacifism. Committed to fighting Hitler and fearful that German scientists were on the verge of developing an atomic bomb, he played a major role in persuading U.S. president Franklin Delano Roosevelt to begin development in the United States of an atomic bomb, which was based in large part on his ideas about the structure of the atom. He remained in Princeton after the war, living and working as quietly as possible, avoiding publicity and autograph seekers as much as he could. Einstein died there on April 18, 1955, leaving behind a body of work comprising some of the greatest scientific discoveries in history.

For More Information

Clark, Ronald W. *Einstein: His Life and Times.* New York: Avon, 1972.

Hoffman, Banesh. *Albert Einstein: Creator and Rebel.* New York: Plume, 1973.

Pagels, Heinz. *The Cosmic Code: Quantum Physics as the Language of Nature.* New York: Simon and Schuster, 1982.

Marie Curie

1867-1934

Personal Background

Maria Salomea Sklodovska was born in Warsaw, Poland, on November 7, 1867. Her parents, Vladislav and Bronislava Sklodovska, were both teachers. The youngest of five children, Maria had three older sisters (Zosia, Bronia, and Hela) and a brother, Jozef. Zosia, her oldest sister, died of typhus when Maria was nine; two years later, her mother died of tuberculosis.

Hard-won education. Like Bronia and Jozef, Maria graduated first in her class at age fifteen. She and her sisters wanted college degrees, but the university in Warsaw admitted only boys. In order to attend college, the girls would have to go abroad—yet their father did not make enough money to send them to a foreign university. So Maria and Bronia agreed to help each other. Maria worked as a nanny for several years, sending money to Bronia while Bronia studied in Paris. At the same time, she read as much as possible in subjects like science—her favorite—and literature. Then, when Bronia had earned her degree, she sent for Maria, ready to help her through school. In 1891, at age twenty-three, Maria packed up her belongings and went to Paris.

Paris. By then Bronia had married a young Polish doctor, and the couple had settled into Paris's large Polish community. They had a busy social life; it seemed that visitors were always stopping by just when Maria needed to study in peace. She soon

▲ **Marie Curie**

Event: Discovering radioactivity.

Role: In 1897 Marie Curie began studying the mineral uranium, which, it had been reported, emitted a mysterious form of energy that appeared as "rays." Working with her husband, Pierre, it occurred to her that this emission took place within the atom itself. Experiments based on her work led to our earliest understanding of the atom's structure, which would ultimately lead to the development of nuclear power and the birth of the atom bomb.

▲ Marie and Pierre Curie in 1896 in their laboratory; the couple worked together from the start of their marriage.

decided to find her own apartment, choosing a tiny room closer to the Sorbonne (the University of Paris). There, for the next few years, she ignored the exciting city around her and delighted in concentrating on her studies.

In July 1893, Marie—she had adopted the French form of her name—placed first among the students taking the exam for science. The next year she placed second in the same exam for mathematics. She began preparing to return to Poland, where her academic success would mean a good job as a teacher.

Pierre Curie. In the spring of 1894, however, Marie met a quiet Frenchman named Pierre Curie. Unconventional, intense, and slightly dreamy, Pierre was thirty-five, nine years older than Marie. Marie had taken a job researching the magnetic properties of steel, and some Polish friends, the Kowalskis, happened to know Pierre. A teacher at the École de Physique et Chimie (School of Physics and Chemistry) in Paris, Pierre had already done important work on magnetism and was now experimenting with crystals. The Kowalskis introduced the two, and soon Pierre was courting Marie. They fell in love and were married in July 1895.

Participation: Discovering Radioactivity

Partnership. The Curies worked together from the start of their marriage, though at first Pierre concentrated on his crystals and Marie on her magnetism. Still, they read the same articles in scientific journals, discussed the articles, and shared notes. Soon they were working together on puzzling problems. This made the two unusually close and their marriage uniquely strong.

In September 1897, Marie gave birth to a baby girl, whom they named Irene. Soon after, she decided to begin work on her doctorate.

X-rays. In 1895, soon after the Curies' marriage, German physicist Wilhelm Roentgen discovered that electricity could produce invisible rays that could pass through some soft objects. On

Love Prevails

Both Marie and Pierre Curie had been in love with someone else before they met. Marie had fallen for the son of a family for whom she had worked in Poland, but the family had objected to her family's social standing; the boy bowed to his family's wishes and ended the relationship. Pierre, for his part, had loved a girl who died when he was twenty. Pierre and Marie had been wounded by love, and each had decided to put science ahead of any future relationships. Still, their attraction to each other was too strong to be ignored—as were their common backgrounds and interests.

a photographic plate, these rays left a shadow picture of hard materials encased in soft ones—for example, bones in tissue. Roentgen took a picture of his wife's hand using the rays; the picture clearly showed her bones and wedding ring, but not the soft tissues of her hand. He called the rays "X-rays" because they were so mysterious. ("X" is often used in mathematics and science to indicate something unknown.)

Uranium rays. The following year, a French physicist named Henri Becquerel accidentally found that a similar effect could be produced on photographic paper by using the mineral uranium. He had left a piece of photographic paper sitting out with a piece of uranium carelessly placed on top of it. The paper had turned cloudy where the uranium had rested.

Irene

By the time she was in her teens, Irene Curie had begun to work closely with her mother. With her husband, Fredrick Joliot, she, too, won a Nobel Prize for work on radioactivity, in 1935.

While X-rays captured great scientific and public attention, Becquerel's uranium rays went largely ignored, perhaps because cloudy paper was not as exciting as the "skeleton" pictures created by X-rays. Even Becquerel himself lost interest soon after his discovery. But his work was exactly what Marie Curie was seeking for her doctoral study: a difficult and interesting phenomenon that no one else was investigating. In December 1897, she decided to begin research on uranium to see if she could explain the source of its strange power.

The puzzle of pitchblende. Pierre helped Marie find a working space at the school where he taught. In this small, unheated room on the school's ground floor, she began her work. She had only a few benches and tables on which to work and the simplest of homemade instruments. The instruments, in fact, had been made by Pierre and his brother Jacques, both skilled mechanics and inventors as well as scientists.

Marie began by testing uranium to see if she could get the same results as Becquerel. She did. She then tested other elements, such as gold and copper. Nothing. Then, in February 1898, she tested a clump of the sticky black mineral compound called pitchblende, in which uranium had first been found. Pitchblende gave Marie Curie her first surprise result.

▲ Marie Curie in her laboratory; by the early twentieth century, science had entered a whole new world, a realm far beyond the daily experiences of most researchers.

Common sense said that pitchblende should give a weaker reading on her instruments than uranium, since the uranium was only one ingredient in the material, and thus its forces would be diluted by the other elements present. Instead, it gave a stronger reading; apparently, the pitchblende was giving off more energy than the uranium alone. It was more active. A few days later, Marie came across another mineral, aeschynite, which was also active, though aeschynite contains no uranium at all. It did contain another mineral, though, called thorium, which when tested alone proved more active than uranium. But pitchblende, the impure mix of minerals, was the most active of all. Why?

By testing thorium Marie had demonstrated that the activity that clouded Becquerel's paper was not restricted to uranium. By spring she was working to separate out, or isolate, other minerals in the pitchblende mixture. In April she suggested that "these minerals may contain a much more active element than uranium" (Quinn, p. 149). She ground the pitchblende up, put it through a sieve, boiled it, distilled it, and finally ran an electric current through it. This tough, physical work succeeded in breaking down the pitchblende.

New elements and atomic insight. As she worked, Marie published her results in scientific journals. "All uranium compounds are active, the more so, in general, the more uranium they contain," she wrote (Quinn, p. 149). This implied that the activity was not a chemical process. That is, it was not occurring because of interactions between uranium and other elements. It seemed to be occurring within the uranium itself—it seemed to be an atomic process. It would be years, however, before this became clear. No one yet understood how atoms worked.

Radiation and the Atom

Radiation takes place when an atom "decays," sending out particles (electrons, protons, neutrons). It took years, however, for science to understand this process. Ultimately, though, knowledge about radiation helped scientists learn more about the atom and its structure. In the early twentieth century, Ernest Rutherford, a New Zealander who lived in England, shot radiation particles at thin metal foil. By studying how some particles bounced off the foil while others passed right through, he could tell that the atom possessed a tiny nucleus (core), which deflected the particles that struck it directly.

By this time, Pierre, realizing the possible importance of Marie's findings, was working closely with her. There was a new element, they suspected, hidden in the pitchblende, making it more active than the uranium. Each time the Curies broke down the pitchblende, they would take the most active part and break it down further. Soon their results revealed that, in fact, the pitchblende contained two such elements, not just one. Before they went on their summer vacation, they had identified one of them, calling it polonium in honor of Marie's native Poland. It was four hundred times more active than uranium, they noted in their report. Using the Latin term for "ray," they called the element "radioactive," a new word to describe something that emits rays.

Later in 1898 (after bicycling around the countryside), the Curies found the second element. They called it radium. Radium was many times more radioactive than even polonium. It would be years before Marie would succeed in coming up with a pure form of radium, but in less than a year the Curies had discovered two new elements and opened a window on the atom.

Nobel Prize. The scientific world was now paying close attention to the Curies' discoveries, and many articles were published challenging their claims. In order to prove their case, they had to produce a purer form of radium. This was Marie's job, breaking down huge amounts of pitchblende and analyzing the results. At the same time, she began teaching two days a week at a girls' school for science just outside of Paris.

Pierre, meanwhile, grew more and more interested in the theoretical side of radioactivity, the question of how it actually worked. Soon other laboratories were confirming the Curies' discoveries. In 1902 Marie managed to refine a tiny amount, one tenth of a gram, of nearly pure radium. The following year Henri Becquerel and the Curies shared the Nobel Prize for physics for their work on radioactivity. It was the third year the prizes had been awarded, and the first time one had been bestowed on a woman.

Wonder Substance

Like X-rays, radium captured the public imagination; its spooky glow intrigued people. It was claimed to have miraculous health-giving properties. Manufacturers of pills and other medicines took advantage of such beliefs, using radium in their products along with advertising claims of its wondrous powers. Only slowly did radium's dangers become known. Today, it is used to treat diseases such as cancer, but only with extreme care. Its radiation works by killing cells (the basic units of living matter from which all plants and animals are built), so doctors must be sure it affects only the cancerous cells, leaving the surrounding ones healthy.

Illness. The Curies discovered almost immediately that the materials they were handling created painful red burns on the hands and other parts of the body that came into contact with them. Indeed, Marie's hands would remain scarred and often cause her pain. We now know that radiation causes other, long-term health problems that may take years to emerge.

Soon after beginning their work, the Curies had begun feeling tired and sick. Both were too ill in 1903 to go to Sweden to accept their Nobel Prize. They blamed the condition on hard work and long hours in the lab, but with hindsight it is clear that they were both suffering from radiation sickness. Later that year, Marie gave birth to a baby who died soon afterward. This, too, seems to have been caused by Marie's exposure to massive doses of radiation.

Tragedy. The Nobel Prize brought the Curies money and worldwide fame (which, they found, often interfered with their work). In 1904 Marie gave birth to another baby girl, Eve. Pierre accepted a top position at the Sorbonne and was elected to the Academy of Sciences, which had turned him down years earlier. Marie won many honors. It was frequently claimed that Pierre had done the important work; the Curies ignored such talk.

Then, in 1906, Pierre was struck by a horse-drawn wagon while crossing the street. His head was crushed under its wheels, which killed him instantly.

The Nobel Prize

The Nobel Prize has been awarded yearly since 1901. The honor is bestowed on individuals or institutions judged to confer "the greatest benefit on mankind" in any one of six fields: physics, chemistry, physiology or medicine, literature, peace, and economics (awards in economics were not handed down until 1969). The awards originate in Sweden—the winner in physics is determined by the Swedish Royal Academy of Science—home of Alfred Bernhard Nobel (1833-1896), who established the Nobel Foundation, which provides the prize money that accompanies the award. Nobel was the inventor of dynamite and other explosives. As a pacifist (one who places peace before all political concerns), he was greatly saddened that his work was used for military purposes.

Aftermath

Collapse and recovery. The sudden and brutal loss of Pierre shattered Marie. Plagued by poor health, her recovery from this enormous grief was very slow. Though she continued to do vital work on radioactivity, the high point of her research—the discovery of radium—was behind her. Often depressed, ill, or exhausted, she nonetheless managed to carry on, finally producing pure radium in 1910. For this achievement, she won her second Nobel Prize, in 1911.

At the same time, others were building on the ground Marie had broken, using radioactivity to map the structure of the atom. By now one of the world's most famous scientists, she replaced Pierre at the Sorbonne, becoming the first woman to teach there.

In 1914 the university finished work on its Radium Institute, established to continue the research she had started. And in 1918, after World War I, she became the institute's director. She remained in the position until her death—from illnesses caused by long-term radiation poisoning—on July 4, 1934.

In 1995 the graves of Pierre and Marie Curie were moved by the French government to the Pantheon in Paris, where France's most honored citizens are buried.

For More Information

Dunn, Andrew. *Marie Curie.* New York: Bookwright, 1991.

Parker, Steve. *Marie Curie and Radium.* New York: Harper, 1992.

Pflaum, Rosalynd. *Marie Curie and Her Daughter Irene.* Minneapolis: Lerner, 1993.

Quinn, Susan. *Marie Curie: A Life.* New York: Simon and Schuster, 1995.

Sigmund Freud

1856-1939

Personal Background

Sigismund Schlomo Freud was born May 6, 1856, in the small Central European village-state of Freiberg, then part of the Austrian empire (now Pribor, in the Czech Republic). His father, Jacob Freud, was descended from German Jews who had migrated eastward centuries earlier to escape anti-Jewish persecution. Amalie Nathanson, Sigmund's mother, was Jacob's third wife; they married in 1855.

Amalie, who was quite beautiful, was nineteen years old—less than half her husband's age—when she married. She came from a Jewish family that had long lived in Central Europe. Amalie met Jacob Freud in Vienna, the Austrian capital. Sigmund, as he would call himself from his teen years, was born the year after Jacob and Amalie married. He had two older half-brothers from his father's first marriage; seven more siblings would be born later.

Family favorite. The Freuds were poor, occupying a single room in a house in Freiberg. When Sigmund was four, the family moved to Vienna, about 150 miles to the southeast. There the family fortunes improved slightly. It was not a highly religious household, though the family's Jewish cultural identity was strong. Amalie Freud adhered closely to Jewish religious practices; her husband did not. Nonetheless, Jacob Freud was proud of his Jewish heritage and education.

▲ **Sigmund Freud**

Event: Developing psychoanalysis.

Role: In his huge body of writings, Sigmund Freud formulated numerous theories about human personality and behavior. His practice of medicine revealed that some illnesses originate in the mind, not the body. Freud called his theories and the "talking cure" he pioneered to help treat his patients psychoanalysis.

Both of Sigmund's parents recognized the boy's unusual intelligence. From an early age, he was openly treated as the family favorite. When his sister's piano practice disturbed his studying, for example, the parents got rid of the piano without a second thought of the girl's interest in music. The fact that Sigmund came first was soon taken for granted by the rest of the family. This left him with a lifelong sense of confidence in his abilities and in his destiny as a man of great accomplishment.

Medicine. A hardworking honors student, Freud placed first in his class in six of his eight years of schooling. Unsure of his future after graduating, he thought about becoming a lawyer, but he soon decided to go into medicine.

Illuminating Childhood

Freud's theories changed forever the way Western culture views childhood, by showing how profoundly childhood experiences characterize the adult who has lived through them. Before Freud, society perceived children basically as small and inexperienced adults. Raising them was a question not of shaping their minds, but of simply filling them with useful knowledge. Freud suggested that a child's mind goes through a series of growth changes, much as their bodies do. Over the years, those who have tried to understand Freud's ideas have looked very closely at his childhood.

In 1873, at seventeen, Freud entered the University of Vienna as a medical student. His focus, however, was still developing, and he took eight years to finish his studies instead of the customary five. He studied zoology for a while, performing detailed research on river eels. Then, in 1876, he began to focus on physiology, the study of the functions of living things. He studied physiology for six years, making it the cornerstone of his medical training. He graduated in 1881, planning to continue his research in physiology.

In 1882, however, Freud met and fell in love with a pretty young woman named Martha Bernays. She agreed to marry him. But Freud knew there was little money in research, probably not enough to support a family. It was time, he decided, to shift from medical research to the practice of medicine.

Participation: Developing Psychoanalysis

Growing interest in psychology. Soon after becoming engaged, Freud accepted a position at Vienna's General Hospital. For three years, he worked in one department after another:

surgery, skin diseases, internal medicine, nervous diseases, psychiatry. Highly ambitious, he looked for a way to combine his interests with a decent income and the promise of advancement. Slowly, he began to focus on the mind, studying the rapidly growing fields of psychology and psychiatry.

Joseph Breuer and "Anna O." At the same time, Freud's friend Joseph Breuer, also a doctor, began telling Freud about a patient he had been treating. A young woman named Bertha Pappenheim, she is known to medical history as "Anna O." (a name Breuer used to protect her identity). She has been called the first patient of psychoanalysis.

In 1880, while caring for her terminally ill father, Bertha Pappenheim had begun suffering from a number of physical complaints: headaches, loss of appetite, weakness, coughing. These symptoms got worse, until she was regularly reporting periods of memory loss, extreme mood swings, and hallucinations involving black snakes, skulls, and skeletons. Sometimes she seemed to have two separate personalities; while normally she could speak French, English, and Italian, at times she could speak only one of these languages. Her father died in April 1881, after which her problems worsened.

"Talking cure." Luckily for Joseph Breuer, Freud, and the future of medicine, Bertha Pappenheim was unusually intelligent and strong willed. (Later she would become famous as a pioneer of women's rights; her identity as "Anna O." was not publicly known until long afterward.) Gradually, during Anna's daily visits, Breuer and Freud discovered that by discussing certain of her memories and the feelings they created in her, some of her symptoms could be made to disappear. Breuer realized that the symptoms had first begun to appear when she held back or "repressed" her reaction to an uncomfortable situation. When Breuer encouraged Anna to

Psyche

Scientists have long used Greek and Latin terms to describe new or developing areas of science. From the Greek word "psyche" (pronounced "**sy** kee"), originally "soul" or "spirit," came labels for several such developing fields in the nineteenth century. Thus, psychology is "the study of the psyche." Psychiatry, a branch of medical science, is the *"healing* of the psyche," or the search for ways to treat mental illness. Freud's method, "psychoanalysis," refers to the "analysis" or "breaking down" of the psyche into its various parts. Freudian psychoanalysts study the psyche, but like psychiatrists, they also try to treat what ails it.

recall the stressful situation and express the reaction she had earlier repressed, her symptoms vanished. The two often used hypnosis during these discussions—Anna would hypnotize herself, or Breuer would hypnotize her. She called it her talking cure.

Breuer first told Freud about "Anna O." in late 1882. Not until a decade later, in the early 1890s, however, did Freud and Breuer, working together, first publish articles about her. In the meantime, Freud had spent two months in 1884 doing research on the drug cocaine and its effects on the mind and body. He had spent five months (1885-86) studying in Paris with Jean-Martin Charcot, a noted authority on the human brain. Charcot impressed Freud with the power of hypnosis. Freud, however, did not impress Charcot with his and Breuer's "talking cure."

Family and patients. Freud had finally married Martha Bernays in 1886 after a long, difficult engagement. At one point, after her parents left Vienna, the couple had been forced to spend two years apart. In October 1887, Martha Freud gave birth to a daughter they named Mathilde, after Joseph Breuer's wife. She was the first of six children; as the others followed in coming years, family life became more and more important to Freud. He soon moved his medical practice to the family home. During his patients' visits, he generally listened as they took part in his "talking cure." Between their visits, he would spend time with his wife and children.

The patients Freud saw often complained of problems similar to Anna O.'s. If he could find no physical reason for the symptoms, such as swelling or tumors in the brain, for example, he would conclude that somehow these physical problems originated in the mind. He soon began to identify a mysterious factor that he felt was central to understanding such problems.

Sex and "hysteria." In most of nineteenth-century Western culture, anything concerning sexual activity was considered dirty and shameful, at least in most social situations. There were strict rules, for example, governing conversation, especially between men and women. Sexual matters were literally unmentionable, and most of the time in public people pretended that sex simply didn't exist. When it was necessary to refer to it, even indirectly, they used polite phrases that disguised the sexual nature of whatever it was they were discussing. This customs persists even today in some social circles.

SIGMUND FREUD

The symptoms that Breuer and Freud had observed in Anna O.'s behavior were not uncommon. They occurred especially in women, but also from time to time in men. Doctors lumped all such symptoms together under the general name "hysteria." In 1895 Freud and Breuer published their work in a book called *Studies in Hysteria.* Freud was now beginning to see sex—or rather, society's attitudes toward sex—as more and more responsible for psychological problems like hysteria. The stress of always holding back or "repressing" sexual memories, thoughts, or impulses, Freud began to believe, created hysterical symptoms. This conclusion made Breuer extremely uncomfortable, and after 1895 he lost interest in further research. Freud, however, was just beginning this line of inquiry.

Self-analysis. As he began to develop his ideas about hysteria and sexual repression, Freud examined his own memories, thoughts, and impulses, effectively becoming his own patient. His "self-analysis," begun in the 1890s, would continue for the rest of his life. Among his findings were many childhood memories that seemed sexual in nature, or violent and aggressive. For example, Freud remembered having a sexual interest in

The Oedipus Complex

The feelings Freud recalled having toward his mother, father, and brother became basic precepts of psychoanalysis. They reveal what he saw as the two strongest factors shaping human behavior: sexuality and aggression. Freud called this sexual attraction to the parent of the opposite sex and jealousy toward the parent of the same sex the Oedipus Complex. The name is based on a Greek play in which Oedipus, the hero of the tragedy, unknowingly kills his father and marries his mother. Freud called feelings of jealousy directed at a brother or sister "sibling rivalry." Like so many of Freud's findings, these terms are now commonly used.

his mother's body as a very young boy. At the same age, he had felt jealousy toward his father. He also recalled feeling violent jealousy toward his younger brother, which resulted in intense feelings of guilt when his brother fell ill and died. Such feelings, he believed, were not unique to him. On the contrary, he was convinced that every child had similar feelings, feelings that were part of being human.

59

▲ Freud set up his medical practice in the family home; between visits with his patients, he would spend time with his wife and children.

The Interpretation of Dreams. In 1899 Freud published *The Interpretation of Dreams,* in which he first laid out the basic principles of psychoanalytic theory. As the title suggests, the book also introduces another idea fundamental to his theory—the importance of dreams. If aggression and sexuality are the two strongest motivations behind our behavior, Freud argues, then dreams are the best clue we have to understanding how these forces are at work in our minds. Dreams, he claims, are messages from our unconscious, the part of our minds of which we are usually unaware.

At first *The Interpretation of Dreams* attracted little attention, even though Freud followed it up with a steady stream of writings in which he continued to develop his ideas. Slowly, however, as these works were read and understood, they won a small but growing following of physicians. Beginning in 1902, this group began meeting at Freud's house every Wednesday evening to discuss his discoveries.

As it grew, this "Psychological Wednesday Circle" became first the Vienna Psycho-Analytical Society in 1908, and then the International Psycho-Analytical Association in 1910. By then its founder had achieved fame throughout the world.

Aftermath

Dissension. Many of Freud's early followers were brilliant men in their own right, however, and disagreements soon arose. The International Psycho-Analytical Association broke up in 1911, as men like Alfred Adler and Carl Jung devoted more time to their own ideas about psychology. Nonetheless, psychoanalysis had become firmly established. Though deeply disappointed by the bitterness that often accompanied these philosophical disagreements, Freud kept up his remarkable pace of writing, lecturing, and treating patients. In 1923 he had the first of many operations for cancer of the jaw, caused by his heavy cigar smoking.

As his health failed with advancing age, Freud's daughter Anna, a psychologist, became his primary assistant and source of support. In 1938, after the Nazis took control of Austria, she helped him move to London. Sigmund Freud died there on September 23, 1939.

For More Information

Freud, Ernst, and others. *Sigmund Freud: His Life in Pictures and Words*. New York: Harcourt Brace, 1978.

Gay, Peter. *Freud: A Life for Our Time*. New York: Anchor Books, 1989.

Gay, Peter, editor. *The Freud Reader*. New York: Norton, 1989.

Edwin Hubble

1889-1953

Personal Background

Edwin Powell Hubble was born on November 20, 1889, in the small Missouri town of Marshfield. His mother and father, Virginia James and John Powell Hubble, were strict disciplinarians. Edwin was the fifth of seven children, and like the others, he earned his own spending money from an early age. The family moved to Kentucky and then Chicago, where Edwin attended high school.

Heavyweight. Even as a boy, Edwin showed a talent for astronomy. But he had many other interests as well, sports ranking high among them. Intelligent and athletic, he did well in school without having to work very hard. When he won a scholarship to the University of Chicago, a teacher reportedly told him, "I have never seen you study for ten minutes" (Whitney, p. 222).

In college, Hubble majored in mathematics and astronomy. He also made the varsity boxing, track, and basketball teams. By then he was six-foot-two, with a square jaw and rugged, handsome features. Hubble was a good enough boxer that one promoter wanted him to fight the heavyweight champion. Hubble, however, had other ideas. In 1910 he went to Oxford University in England on a Rhodes scholarship. There he studied law (and boxed against the French champion), returning to the United States to open a law practice in Louisville, Kentucky in 1913.

▲ Edwin Hubble

Event: Discovering galaxies beyond the Milky Way; establishing the big-bang theory.

Role: American astronomer Edwin Hubble discovered that there are galaxies in the universe other than our own Milky Way, and that galaxies are moving away from each other. His work later resulted in the "big-bang theory," a view of the universe's origins that has now won general acceptance.

"Off to war." Bored with a lawyer's life, however, Hubble soon decided to "chuck the law for astronomy" (Whitney, p. 222). He returned to the University of Chicago to earn a doctorate in astronomy, writing his thesis on the faint and fuzzy celestial objects called nebulas (clouds of gas or dust).

The United States entered World War I just as Hubble finished his degree, and in 1917 he joined the army. Because of this he had to temporarily turn down an invitation from the great astronomer George Ellery Hale to work at the Mt. Wilson Observatory in California. "Regret cannot accept your invitation. Am off to war" (Berendzen, p. 206), the young man telegraphed Hale. After achieving the rank of major and being wounded in battle, Hubble returned from Europe in the summer of 1919. He then accepted the position at Mt. Wilson.

Nebula Debate

The term nebula (Latin for cloud) has a controversial history. The designation originally included many objects first viewed as virtually indistinguishable fuzzy blobs of light but which later (with better telescopes) turned out to be distinctly different from one another. In the early twentieth century, astronomers argued fiercely over nebulas. Some thought that certain nebulas might be separate galaxies outside of our own galaxy, the Milky Way. Others insisted that our galaxy was the only one. Hubble's discoveries with the new 100-inch telescope settled the debate, proving that there were indeed other galaxies beyond the Milky Way.

Participation: Discovering Galaxies Beyond the Milky Way; Establishing the Big-Bang Theory

Mt. Wilson. Located in Southern California's San Gabriel Mountains, high above the city of Pasadena, the observatory at Mt. Wilson had recently been upgraded by the completion of a powerful new telescope. With this telescope, which featured a 100-inch mirror, Hubble would make his pioneering observations. He would remain at Mt. Wilson throughout his career, overseeing completion of a 200-inch telescope in the late 1940s.

The 100-inch telescope, the most powerful of its day, was just coming into use as Hubble arrived at Mt. Wilson. It was a lucky combination of human ingenuity and instrument. The large mirror gathered just enough light to bring some of the little-understood nebulas into focus. This new visual information challenged Hubble's determination to understand what he was seeing.

"Island universes." The key to Hubble's discovery of other galaxies (systems that contain stars, gas, dust, and planets) beyond our own lay in a class of stars called variables. Variables got their name because their light output changes over time, varying between dim and bright. In 1912 astronomer Henrietta Leavitt discovered that the light pulses of some variable stars could allow astronomers to figure out how far away they are. By the early 1920s, Hubble was turning the powerful Mt. Wilson telescope on the nebulas he had studied while earning his doctorate.

On October 5, 1923, Hubble took a photo of a distant nebula in which, after long hours of study, he found a variable star that he felt could tell him how far away it was. Some of the nebular objects in this faraway mass had earlier appeared to be clusters of stars. These clusters were thought to be within our own Milky Way Galaxy. Hubble could test this belief by using the variable.

For the first time, it was discovered how far away a nebula was—and it was much too far away to be inside our own galaxy. Soon Hubble found many other variables in the same nebula, which is now called the Andromeda Galaxy. Hubble had settled the great nebula debate—there were indeed other galaxies outside of ours, "island universes," as they were also called. We know today that billions of them make up the universe.

Henrietta Leavitt and Cepheid Variables

In an age when men dominated universities, Harvard astronomer Henrietta Leavitt was given the relatively dull task of examining routine photos. Her hours of study, however, brought a major discovery. In the photos were a type of pulsing star called Cepheid (pronounced "**seh** fee id") variables, which have a regular pattern of brightness and dimness, and keep to a tight schedule of light variation. Leavitt noticed a direct link between a Cepheid's schedule and its overall brightness: the longer the periods of brightness and dimness, the brighter the star is overall. She also knew that far-away stars seem dimmer than closer ones. By comparing how bright a Cepheid appears to be with how bright its schedule says it actually is, she suggested, we can figure out its distance from earth. Leavitt thus made Cepheid variables into the distance markers of the universe.

Classifying galaxies. In 1925, having proved the existence of galaxies beyond our own, Hubble introduced a system of classifying them, or breaking them down into types of galaxies. Most he divided into two main groups. Spiral galaxies, like the Milky Way, have huge arms that trail around a rotating center. Others,

▲ Hubble in 1931 with an early model of the 200-inch Hale telescope at the Mt. Palomar Observatory. In 1948, when the telescope was completed, Hubble was the first to use it.

the "elliptical" galaxies, also rotate around a center, but are shaped like saucers, lacking the arms of the spiral galaxies.

Red shift. Hubble continued his pioneering work on galaxies throughout the 1920s, determining distances for over twenty galaxies surrounding the Milky Way. In 1929 this work led to his most important discovery. For over a decade, scientists had predicted that the light coming from some distant galaxies might indicate that the galaxies were moving apart from each other and Earth. If the galaxies were speeding fast enough away from earth, the motion would "stretch" the light waves emitting from them. Since longer wavelengths make light take on a reddish tone, this stretching was called the "red shift."

The mathematics for predicting red shifts were based on the general theory of relativity, published in 1916 by physicist **Albert Einstein** (see entry) and extended in the 1920s by other mathematicians. General relativity held that gravity is not so much a *force* as it is *geometry*—the geometry of space. Big objects like planets bend the space around them; smaller objects simply follow the bending of space.

Some astronomers had actually reported red shifts in the light from nebulas as early as 1912. But no one then really knew what nebulas were, or how large or distant they were. As a result, it was too early to draw conclusions about their movement.

Expanding universe. Hubble's greatest achievement was to determine the red shifts for a large number of galaxies by measuring the wavelengths of the light coming from them. His measurements led him to two important conclusions. First, distant galaxies did seem to be moving away from Earth. Second, the farther away they were from Earth, the faster they seemed to move. This relationship between a galaxy's distance and its speed is now known as Hubble's law.

At first glance, this observation of the movement of galaxies relative to Earth might make it seem that Earth was somehow the center of the universe. Instead, though, the motion of the galaxies can be explained by an idea based on Einstein's theory of relativity: the expansion of space itself. It is not so much that the galaxies are moving by themselves, according to this idea; rather, they are moving along with the expanding space around them.

Big bang. One of the basic questions about the universe has always been its age. How old is everything? Or is the universe actually ageless, without a beginning or an end? Thanks to Hubble's observations, scientists had a way of starting to answer these seemingly unanswerable questions. For if the universe were expanding, they figured, that expansion had to start somewhere. Aleksandr Friedman and Georges Lemaitre, the mathematicians who had extended Einstein's work in the 1920s, had found that relativity suggested an origin for the universe. That origin, they said, was a single point from which the universe had first expanded. From this tiny point—known as a singularity—space, time, and matter (or material substance; virtually everything in the universe is made up of matter) expanded into being.

This idea was highly controversial. Leading cosmologists argued against it. They suggested instead that the universe exists in a "steady state," without beginning or end, in which expansion comes from the constant creation of new matter. Taking the position opposite the "steady-staters" were scientists like George Gamow, who came up with the term "big bang" in 1946 to describe the universe's earliest expansion.

Hubble himself stayed out of such cosmological arguments. Dignified and gentlemanly, he puffed a pipe and spoke with a slight British accent, picked up in his three years at Oxford. He viewed his role as simply one of observing and reporting what he observed. For example, he described the galaxies as only *appearing* to be moving according to his measurements. He left it to others to claim that that was what they were *actually* doing.

Palomar. By the 1930s, Hubble had firmly established himself as America's leading astronomer. He was at this time in

Birth of Modern Cosmology

The movement of galaxies is often explained by comparing the universe to the surface of a polka-dotted balloon. As the balloon is inflated, each dot on its surface moves away from the others. The farther one dot is from another, the faster they move away from each other. No one dot is the center of the surface, which has no "center"—instead, the whole surface is expanding.

The theory of relativity suggests that the universe is like the surface of the balloon. By bringing relativity into astronomy in this way, Hubble ushered in an entirely new age in astronomy, humankind's study of the universe (the cosmos) as a whole. Beginning in the 1930s and 1940s, many astronomers and physicists became cosmologists, scientists whose subject was the universe.

▶
Hubble in 1949; Hubble's greatest achievement was to determine the red shifts for a large number of galaxies by measuring the wavelengths of the light coming from them.

charge of the Mt. Wilson Observatory, a father figure to a whole generation of astronomers who studied there. They read his books and articles, including his volume about galaxies, *The Realm of the Nebulae* (1936). Many of them imitated his way of talking and manner.

During the 1930s and 1940s, Hubble was closely involved in the planning and construction of a new 200-inch telescope at Mt. Palomar, another Southern California observatory not far from Mt. Wilson. It was called the Hale telescope, after Hubble's mentor at Mt. Wilson, George Ellery Hale. During World War II, Hubble worked for the army as the head of a research department, and in 1948, when the Hale telescope was completed, he was the first to use it.

In the late 1940s Hubble began suffering from heart problems. On September 28, 1953, he died suddenly, while preparing for a four-night observing session at Mt. Palomar.

Aftermath

Opening the universe. Hubble's work led to the biggest changes in humanity's view of the universe since the time of Polish astronomer Copernicus, who in the sixteenth century had destroyed the old earth-centered version of the solar system. (The solar system includes the Sun and all the celestial objects that move in orbits around it. Before Copernicus, people believed that the Sun orbited around Earth; now we know that Earth orbits around the Sun.)

The astounding scale and organization of the universe has been opened to human understanding by concepts based on Hubble's work. We now have an idea of our place in the universe: we live on a planet orbiting a star in a huge galaxy, one galaxy of the "local group" of galaxies, which is part of larger "cluster" of galaxies, which in turn belongs to one of countless "superclusters," gigantic strings of galaxies spread out across the universe.

Over the years, scientists have made discoveries that strongly support the big-bang theory of how the universe began.

Indeed, what is thought to be leftover heat from the big bang itself was detected in the early 1990s. This so-called cosmic background radiation, measured by extremely sensitive instruments, is widely viewed as final confirmation of the big bang.

Space telescope. Perhaps the most fitting recognition of Edwin Hubble's role in astronomy is the Hubble Space Telescope, the first telescope to be launched into space (in 1990). There, free of Earth's atmosphere, the powerful instrument is able to obtain a crystal-clear view, a look deeper into the universe than humankind has ever had before. Among the Hubble Telescope's discoveries have been what is thought to be a massive black hole at the center of our galaxy and the first evidence of planets orbiting around a distant star.

For More Information

Berendzen, Richard, and others. *Man Discovers the Galaxies.* New York: Neal Watson Academic Publications, Inc., 1976.

Christianson, Gale. *Edwin Hubble: Mariner of the Nebulae.* New York: Farrar, Straus, 1995.

Goldsmith, Donald. *The Astronomers.* New York: St. Martin's, 1991.

Whitney, Charles. *The Discovery of Our Galaxy.* New York: Knopf, 1971.

Hubble Telescope Helps Reveal Black Holes

A black hole is believed to represent the final stage of a massive star's life, when the gravitational force of the star causes it to collapse inward on itself; at the center of the black hole are the densely packed remains of the star. The gravitational field of a black hole is so intense that nothing, not even light, can escape it. Black holes, if they exist, can be detected by their gravitational effects on other heavenly bodies. It has been suggested that the end of the universe will be its becoming a single black hole. With the help of the Hubble Telescope, astronomers have identified a number of possible black holes, but none as yet has been fully confirmed.

Expanding Global Communications

1901

Lee De Forest challenges Italian inventor Guglielmo Marconi in a battle of wireless telegraphy.

1910

De Forest broadcasts music and voice on radio.

1908

Henry Ford introduces the Model T.

1903

Wilbur and **Orville Wright** make their first flights in a powered aircraft.

1914-18

World War I.

1924

Vladimir Zworykin introduces the kinescope.

1939

Zworykin develops the electron microscope.

1933

Nazis take control of Germany.

c. 1925

De Forest unveils a method for making sound motion pictures.

EXPANDING GLOBAL COMMUNICATIONS

The second industrial revolution. By the third quarter of the nineteenth century, the world was in the midst of a second industrial revolution. This time the revolution was driven by expanding world markets and by the development of petroleum and electrical fuels, which spawned a wide array of new machines and technologies. Hundreds, then thousands of products became available to masses of urban workers. At the same time, the demand for shares in the global market demanded improved lines of communication.

Even before this second industrial revolution was under way, better methods of reaching far-flung markets had been invented; for example, Samuel Morse had established telegraph communications by 1844. Alexander Graham Bell produced and demonstrated the telephone in 1876. The race was on to move into the twentieth century with worldwide communications.

Several major problems remained, however; one was how to harness new sources of energy in order to make their power available over great distances. Thomas Edison had captured electricity and made it perform a wide range of activities—if these activities took place near a power plant. Edison's early inventions reduced energy waste in their direct current systems by employing low voltage; but this created an electrical current that could only be carried a short distance. City users could make use of Edison's electric lights or phonographs if they were not too many miles from a power source.

Then, in 1893, Nikola Tesla found a better way to produce and use electrical energy that would eliminate the wasteful sparks of the direct current generators. Tesla developed a way to produce and transmit *alternating* current. With the sparks no longer wasted, electricity flow was increased and could now be sent long distances using high-voltage systems. Alternating current generators were used to create a new world of electronic communication tools. First the wireless telegraph (1895) and then radio (1910) made long-distance communication widely available.

Twentieth-century communications. The century began with automobiles traveling on an improving road system, and with dreamers longing to realize Leonardo da Vinci's fifteenth-century vision of human flight. On a windy day in December 1903, two bicycle repairmen from Ohio, **Wilbur** and **Orville Wright,** became the first successful pilots of a powered craft—a biplane they had carefully designed and built themselves. Their four flights, totaling a little over eight-hundred feet, opened the door to modern airplane flight.

While the Wrights were producing and flying their first airplane, another inventor was studying the possibilities of wireless communication—radio. **Lee De Forest**'s invention of the three-poled (triode) tube allowed radio waves to be amplified so that sound—even music and the human voice—could be transmitted over long distances. Although so many people were investigating radio at the turn of the twentieth century that credit for any innovation is foggy, De Forest's triode led the way to modern radio and, later, television.

Television, the ability to send pictures over the air waves, was not a new idea; it was first suggested in 1874. But a reliable means of broadcasting television images had to wait for a brilliant Russian who had turned to the United States after the Russian Revolution of 1917—**Vladimir Zworykin.** With Zworykin as laboratory director, the electronics giant RCA introduced his kinescope in 1929 and went on to patent a large number of tools for television. Zworykin then turned the laboratory toward other pursuits, developing the electron microscope.

The work of these men, De Forest, the Wright brothers, and Zworykin, and many more discoverers, led to a worldwide communications system.

Wilbur Wright

1867-1912

Orville Wright

1871-1948

Personal Background

Wilbur Wright was born in 1867 near Millville, Indiana; his younger brother, Orville, was born in Dayton, Ohio, in 1871. They had two older brothers named Reuchlin and Lorin, and a younger sister named Katharine. Their father, Milton Wright, was a bishop in the United Brethren in Christ Church. Later in life, he would become a theology professor and editor of a weekly religious newspaper in Dayton. He was a very studious man, but also a dreamer. The boys' mechanical aptitude, however, came from their mother, Susan. She was inventive and good with tools, once single-handedly building a sled for her children.

Newspaper publishers. When Orville was fourteen, he and a friend set up a printing shop in his friend's basement. They began a school newspaper called *Midget* and circulated their own articles and features. Two years later, Orville built his own printing press. After Wilbur made several improvements to the design, the two began printing the church newspaper.

With another homebuilt press, the Wright brothers published the *West Side News,* with Orville as business manager and

▲ **Orville and Wilbur Wright**

Event: Achieving powered flight.

Role: Though not the only ones to attempt powered flight, the Wright brothers were the first to conduct serious wind tunnel experiments, which enabled them to predict how a plane would fly through the air. Because of their methodical observations and sharp mechanical skills—not to mention a relentless determination—they succeeded in building the first working airplane.

Wilbur as editor. The *West Side News* began as a weekly but eventually evolved into a daily paper, *The Evening Item*. When that venture failed, the Wright brothers established a business printing religious pamphlets. Among the men they worked for was Paul Lawrence Dunbar, a friend of Orville's and publisher of *The Tatler,* a newspaper for the black community of Dayton. Dunbar would later become famous as a poet.

Bicycle repairmen. In their early twenties, Wilbur and Orville ran a bicycle repair shop in Dayton. Within three years, they were manufacturing their own models. The business was profitable and kept them busy, but their inventive minds drove them to work on other projects; besides making continual improvements to the bicycle, they made refinements to adding machines and typewriters. Orville even toyed with the idea of starting an automobile manufacturing business. Wilbur, however, thought it was a bad idea—it would be easier to build a flying machine.

A Toy Helicopter

When Orville and Wilbur were seven and eleven, respectively, their father came home with a surprise for them: a toy helicopter powered by a rubber band. The boys were amazed with the bamboo-and-paper toy, which had been created by the French inventor Alphonse Penaud. They tried to make a larger version of the toy, thinking that it would fly higher. Instead, they discovered that the opposite was true: the larger their helicopter model, the more trouble it had flying. This surprised the boys considerably and led to some of their earliest musings on flight.

Building a flying machine. The Wright brothers had heard of glider experiments on both sides of the Atlantic; Otto Lilienthal in Germany and Octave Chanute in the United States were considered pioneers in aviation; they were heroes in the eyes of the bicycle-manufacturing brothers from Dayton. In 1896 Orville came down with typhoid fever. It was during his long recovery that he and Wilbur began to discuss the possibility of building their own glider.

The prospect excited the brothers, and they read everything they could find on the subject. They even wrote the Smithsonian Institution for additional information on gliders. (The Smithsonian is a center for scientific and artistic culture, sponsored by the U.S. government.) The Smithsonian responded with a list of current books on flight, including Chanute's *Progress in Flying Machines* and Samuel P. Langley's *Experiments in Aerodynamics.*

▲ The Wright brothers testing one of their gliders at Kitty Hawk in 1901. Their first glider was a biplane that featured a space for the operator to lie flat and operate the wings. Initially they flew it like a kite, tethered by a rope tied to its nose.

Taking lessons from birds. One of the central problems with glider flight was balance. Glider pioneers were able to keep their wings balanced by shifting their weight to the left or right as

WILBUR WRIGHT

ORVILLE WRIGHT

needed; this was a tiring activity, though, and required near-acrobatic skill.

Watching buzzards, Wilbur noticed that birds keep their balance during flight by changing the curvature of their wings. From this he decided that a working airplane would have to do the same with its wings—that somehow, the wings should be able to alter their shape in flight. One day, while fiddling with an empty cardboard box at the shop, he saw how this could be done.

How Planes Fly

An airplane obtains lift from the aerodynamic effect of the air rushing over its wings. (Aerodynamics concern the flow of air or other gases around a body in motion.) Lift occurs because the wing's upper surface is more convex (curved), and therefore longer, than the lower surface of the wing. As a result, air must travel faster past the upper surface than past the lower, which leads to reduced pressure above the wing. Since the pressure below the wing is stronger than that above, the plane is pushed aloft. The lift provided by the wings must equal the aircraft's weight; the forward thrust of the engine must balance the forces of drag on the plane that result from its movement through the air. In modern flight, there are many other factors to consider as well, but most important is that all the forces act on an airplane's balance.

In the summer of 1899, the Wright brothers built a large kite in the form of a biplane (a plane with two main supporting surfaces, usually placed one above the other), with wings they could control from the ground. By changing the shape of the wing from the ground, they were able to make the kite climb or dive. Once they could successfully control the kite, the brothers decided to build a glider. They began looking for a site to conduct test flights.

Kitty Hawk. In December 1899, Orville and Wilbur wrote to the Weather Bureau for information about wind velocity in different locations. Specifically, they were seeking a place with good weather, fifteen-mile-per-hour winds, and a sandy, treeless terrain. The Weather Bureau recommended Kitty Hawk—a small fishing town on a strip of sand, just off the mainland of North Carolina. In September of the following year, Wilbur and Orville made their first six-hundred-mile trip to Kitty Hawk, leaving their mechanic, Charley Taylor, to look after their bicycle shop. They brought a tent in which to live, a workbench, tools, and their glider.

Their first glider was a biplane that featured a space for the operator to lie flat and operate the wings. Initially the Wrights flew it like a kite, tethered by a rope tied to its nose. Finally, Wilbur got into the craft and let Orville raise him up into the wind. When the wind picked him eight feet off the ground, he began to shout to be let down. Orville, thinking he was cheering to be raised higher, let out more rope. Their experiments with the first glider were a mixed success.

The brothers returned to Kitty Hawk the following year, 1901, with a new glider, a larger model built according to information published by Samuel P. Langley and Otto Lilienthal. They expected the new glider to provide enough lift to easily take them into the air in a strong wind, but this glider performed poorly.

To test the data they had used, the Wright brothers built a small wind tunnel in their bicycle shop. It was an eight-foot-long wooden box, with a metal fan powered by a two-cylinder gas engine they had made themselves. In this box they tested over two hundred different types of wing surfaces. From these experiments, they found that the information on which they'd relied was not merely inaccurate—it was useless.

> ### Theoretically Impossible
>
> Despite the Wrights' success with gliders, and other glider experiments around the world, many of America's foremost scientific experts believed that powered flight was theoretically impossible. Professor Simon Newcomb, a leading mathematician, wrote in 1902 that building an aerial vehicle that would carry a single man would require the discovery of a new metal, or a new force.

For the next two years the Wrights compiled all their own data and used these findings to build a third glider in 1902. This craft, with a wingspan of 32 feet and a wing area of 305 square feet, broke all previous records for glider flight. The Wrights were ready to try powered flight.

Participation: Achieving Powered Flight

No engine light enough. At first, the Wrights assumed that an automobile engine would be suitable for mounting on their glider. Not finding one light enough to meet their specifications, however, they built their own. With the help of Charley Taylor, they designed a small, lightweight four-cylinder engine that could generate twelve horsepower (a unit of power equal to 746 watts,

▲ **The Wright brothers fly at Kitty Hawk on December 17, 1903; Orville was at the controls, Wilbur on the ground.**

named for the power that a horse exerts in pulling). Finding no complete data on screw propellers, the brothers conducted their own experiments with propellers—often riding a bicycle through Dayton with a propeller attached to the front of the bike to see how it would spin in the wind.

When finished, the Wright Flyer I biplane had a wingspan of 40 feet and wing area of 510 square feet. With two engine-driven propellers, it sat on sled runners. The Wrights took this plane to Kitty Hawk in late September, and for three months they worked toward perfecting it, while at the same time flying their old glider. Finally, on December 14, the Wrights laid a track on the slope of Kill Devil Hill to act as a runway. They were ready for their first powered flight.

Wilbur got to fly first, winning a coin toss. The plane got off the ground for three seconds before falling. It had traveled 105 feet—the first true powered flight—but the brothers were disappointed in the short duration of the flight. Then, too, the flight had damaged the plane's left wing. By the time the plane was repaired, two days had passed. This time it was Orville's turn to fly.

Making history. It was a cold morning, with gale-force gusts of wind. The brothers should have postponed the next flight, but they had promised their father and sister that they would return to Dayton in time for Christmas dinner. Orville took off into a twenty-seven-mile-per-hour wind and flew erratically for twelve seconds, traveling 120 feet before crashing in the sand. They tried again. In all, the Wright brothers made four flights that day, the longest by Wilbur—852 feet in just under a minute. They ended their experiments before noon, December 17, 1903, now considered one of the greatest days in history.

Heated Arguments

One of the ways the Wright brothers made decisions was through vigorous, heated argument. As they had agreed years prior, it was the duty of each to attack the other's ideas. Through this method, which constantly forced them to reexamine and defend their thinking, the brothers made sure their ideas were sound.

Most newspapers in the country refused to report the story; too many crackpot inventors had made bogus claims of flight in the past. And since the weight of authority had come down against the possibility of flight, the public was now skeptical, too. Even *Scientific American,* upon getting word of the Wrights' work in 1905, flatly claimed that the only successful flying done that year was in a balloon. A year later, the magazine apologized.

A military invention. In 1904 and 1905, the Wrights improved their plane, making over 120 flights in a friend's 70-acre field outside Dayton. As their flights became smoother and more predictable—from a combination of improved design and better flying skills—they realized that their airplane could be of military significance. Their third biplane, the 1905 Flyer III, was the world's first practical airplane—it could carry two people and remain in the air for over half an hour, performing feats like sharp turns and figure eights.

The British government sent a representative from their War Department. The French sent a military commission. Both governments were interested in the military applications of the new invention. But, being patriots, the Wrights wanted the U.S. Army to have exclusive use of the airplane's military potential. They wrote the army with a contract offer but received an astonishing reply: the army did not believe they could fly.

It wasn't until the beginning of 1908 that the Wrights were able to get an army contract. Even then, it was only because the brothers were already negotiating the sale of the airplane to foreign governments.

Tragedy. In September 1908, during army test flights at Fort Myer, Virginia, one of the Wrights' passengers was killed in a crash; Lt. Thomas Selfridge, who had asked the War Department to let him be a passenger in Orville's tests, died of a fractured skull hours after a cracked propeller forced the plane down in an accident that also broke Orville's left leg and several ribs. Only after news of the crash reached the press and was widely reported was the American public finally convinced that powered flight had been achieved. (An air force base in Michigan is named after Selfridge.)

Aftermath

At the time of Orville's crash, Wilbur was in Europe negotiating with the French government. He flew for thousands of excited French spectators and became a national hero. After Orville's recovery, he and their sister Katharine sailed for Europe, where they were received by European royalty. The French Wright Company began giving flying lessons, and by World War I, airplanes were commonplace all over Europe.

Still, the brothers did not receive recognition at home. The Smithsonian Institution could not admit that two uneducated bicycle salesmen could accomplish, for less than $1,000, what their esteemed secretary could not do with fifty times as much money. It wasn't until 1942 that the Smithsonian made a formal apology, by which time Wilbur had long been dead; he had died of typhoid fever in May 1912. Orville, who had survived the disease years before, sold the family company in 1915. He outlived his brother by thirty-six years.

For More Information

Crouch, Tom D. *The Bishop's Boys: A Life of the Wright Brothers.* New York: W. W. Norton, 1989.

Heyn, Ernest V. *Fire of Genius: Inventors of the Past Century.* New York: Anchor Press/Doubleday, 1976.

Howard, Fred. *Wilbur & Orville: A Biography of the Wright Brothers.* New York: Knopf, 1987.

Those Inventive Americans. Washington, D.C.: National Geographic Society, 1971.

Lee De Forest

1873-1961

Personal Background

Son of a minister. Lee De Forest was born in Council Bluffs, Iowa, in 1873. He was the second of three children of a Congregational minister. When Lee was six, his father was named president of one of the first black colleges in America. Located in Talladega, a small town in Alabama, the struggling new school was created for the education of the children of former slaves. In 1879 Henry Swift De Forest moved his family to Talladega.

As a white boy attending the all-black lower school of the college, and perhaps because he was the son of the college's president, Lee did not have many friends at the school. At the same time, his family was shunned by the white community of Talladega; the Civil War was still a recent event, and the De Forests' neighbors were quite resentful of the Yankees (northerners) who had come to educate the blacks. Thus socially isolated, the middle De Forest child lost himself in the books he found at the college library.

Young inventor. Lee was especially interested in anything mechanical; he avidly read the *Patent Office Official Gazette,* already thinking of himself as an inventor. Soon he was designing steam hammers (large hammering machines that used steam power) and attempting to invent perpetual motion machines

▲ Lee De Forest

Event: Developing radio.

Role: With his invention of the triode tube, Lee De Forest made wireless radio transmission practical. Throughout the course of his career, he secured more than three hundred patents for inventions related to communications.

(machines that would run on their own power forever) of his own. When he was ten or eleven, he wanted to know how a locomotive reversed directions. He walked to a nearby railroad yard and inspected a locomotive. He traced the connections from the reversing lever in the cab through the entire system, over and over again, until he figured out how the system operated. Back at home, Lee enlisted the help of his younger brother to build a wooden version of the locomotive, made from junk but complete with a reverse lever. The enormous contraption actually worked, and it won a certain measure of respect from the neighbors who had shunned the family.

A Shady Side

After later successes, it was revealed that De Forest used unscrupulous means to obtain research funds for some of his ventures. He was sued repeatedly for fraud and claimed that his company's directors were stealing funds. Two of his business associates eventually spent time in jail.

When Lee was old enough for high school, his father sent him to a small boarding school in Mount Hermon, Massachusetts. There, surrounded by farm boys, he became even more withdrawn. When he was fifteen, he wrote a letter to his father, who had hoped the young man would follow in his footsteps and become a minister. In it Lee declared that he intended to become a machinist and inventor. He then asked his father to reconsider where he was being sent to school. He wanted to attend the Sheffield Scientific School at Yale University. His father responded irritably, saying Lee's plan would provide a half-baked education. Nevertheless, he reluctantly agreed to his son's wishes.

Yale. By the time he entered college, on a scholarship, De Forest was by his own admission an extremely timid and unsocial student. He tried to join in student activities—attempting to become editor of the campus magazine and entering design contests—but all of his efforts were failures.

After receiving his degree in 1896, De Forest stayed at Yale for a doctorate, studying the mysterious electromagnetic waves Heinrich Hertz had discovered a decade earlier. Upon receiving his doctorate, he went to work in the field of telephone research for Western Electric in Chicago. He was soon fired, however, for inattention to duty. But when De Forest heard about Italian inventor Guglielmo Marconi and the wireless telegraph he had invented, he knew he had found a pursuit to which he could commit himself fully. (A telegraph is an electrical apparatus for sending coded messages.)

The call of radio. De Forest wrote Marconi asking for a job, but he received no response. Undaunted, in 1899 he went to the international America's Cup yachting races, where Marconi had set up his wireless machine to report the event. De Forest inspected it carefully, noting ways the invention could be improved.

Between 1901 and 1906, De Forest took out thirty-four patents, but none of them had any impact on the emerging field of radio. In addition, with borrowed money, he designed and built equipment for reporting the 1901 yacht races on behalf of the Publishers' Press Association. He had invited Marconi to appear with his system, but neither man's equipment worked. Instead, the signals only jammed each other.

> ## A Hazardous Activity
>
> Some of the equipment early radio researchers used was dangerous; frequently, powerful electrical sparks were generated by primitive, kerosene-filled condensers (an apparatus in which electricity is temporarily stored), each weighing about a ton; any miscalculation could blow up the condenser or electrocute anyone who came too near. In the haphazard atmosphere that prevailed, accidents were common.

In business. In 1902 De Forest and a stock promoter organized a company called the American De Forest Wireless Telegraph Company. He found that he could raise money by demonstrating his ability to send wireless Morse code signals, which by then he could transmit a distance of six miles. He wanted to do the same with telephony—sending voices over the air, without wires.

Participation: Developing Radio

The early years of radio were marked by intense trial and error—not just by De Forest, but by many other American and European inventors working on improving the same kind of system. They frequently repeated experiment after experiment, testing any method that came to mind, with little understanding of the fundamental principles behind their equipment or tests. Ultimately, the breakthrough in radio would be the result of an observation noted

Definitions

Alternating current: a regular flow of electrons first in one direction and then another.

Diaphragm: a thin plate that moves back and forth in a machine such as a telephone receiver to create sound waves.

Direct current: a regular flow of electrons always in the same direction.

Electrode plate: a flat metal plate from which electricity enters or leaves a tube.

Electrons: small parts of atoms having a negative electrical charge.

Feedback: the process of recycling part of the output of a system to become part of the input, thus strengthening the input.

Filament: a very fine, threadlike part.

High-vacuum pump: a pump capable of removing almost all the air from a vessel such as an electronic tube.

Input: power or signal fed into an electric device.

Re-amplify: to increase the strength of an electric current or a sound again.

Spark gap: the space through which an electrically generated spark moves.

Vacuum tube: an electric tube from which almost all air has been removed.

by inventor Thomas Edison a generation earlier.

The Edison effect. In 1883, while experimenting with light bulbs, Thomas Edison discovered that if he put a positively charged wire into a vacuum tube along with a regular filament, electricity would flow from the filament to the wire. Although he made note of this curious phenomenon, he never pursued it. Twenty years passed before the phenomenon, later called the "Edison effect," was explored further.

The triode. In 1906, while experimenting with various designs of the vacuum tube, De Forest turned British physicist John Ambrose Fleming's diode (an electronic valve with two electrodes) into a triode by adding a grid between the filament and the plate. The grid was just a bent piece of wire located between the two already present electrodes and connected to an outer antenna—but it possessed an amazing property: it greatly amplified (built up) the signal being received. The triode was patented by De Forest on January 15, 1907.

What De Forest had found, through trial and error, was a method of amplifying the tiny amount of energy that flowed through the air and could be captured by an antenna. By connecting the antenna to the grid of his triode, the small fluctuations in electrical current were boosted to a signal strong enough to power a speaker. De Forest called his triode the "Audion" tube.

De Forest's triode was of little commercial use as long as the metals inside the tube were susceptible to rust. When a good high-vacuum pump became available two years later, it was found

▲ De Forest in his laboratory in 1907; with his invention of the triode tube, Lee De Forest made wireless radio transmission practical.

that a better vacuum not only prevented rust—it significantly improved the performance of the tube. With this knowledge in hand, De Forest continued his research.

The regenerative circuit. Soon De Forest and others discovered that by changing the circuitry of the tube to reconnect part of the output back into the input, it was possible to "feed back" and thus re-amplify the signal. This advance, called the feedback or regenerative circuit, proved to be an efficient method of producing

91

strong electromagnetic waves that could be used to carry a wider range of sound. Until that time, wireless transmission was only possible with spark gaps—useful for Morse code communications but not much more. The regenerative circuit finally made it possible to transmit any type of sound over the air, including music and the human voice.

Marriage. In 1906 De Forest met his first wife while installing a radio in her house. He courted her over the airwaves from his own transmitter, and the newspapers reported the world's first electronic courtship. But the resulting marriage, like two subsequent ones, did not last.

Entrepreneur. On January 13, 1910, De Forest broadcast the voices of opera stars from New York, using his refined Audion tube. The concert featured the famous tenor Enrico Caruso and was picked up by many people over a wide area. The American Telephone and Telegraph Company (AT&T) soon bought the telephone rights to the Audion tube for $50,000, and Western Electric paid $150,000 for the radio rights. With the money he made on the sale of rights to his triode, De Forest started another company in New York, which began to manufacture tubes and equipment for the military.

By 1917 the refined Audion tube was commercially available to consumers, who were becoming more and more interested in radio as a hobby.

Aftermath

Hollywood. In the 1920s, De Forest lost interest in the Audion tube and in radio altogether. He sold his company in 1923 and moved to Hollywood, having become intrigued by the idea of sound movies. He developed a sound-on-picture system that worked by printing a soundtrack on the film itself. He called his system "phonofilm" and tried to sell it to the major Hollywood studios. At the time, none were interested.

In 1927 the first sound movie was released, but only as a last-ditch gimmick to save the Warner Brothers film studio from bankruptcy. The first "talkie," though, did not use De Forest's "phonofilm" system. Instead, it used a much cruder approach, synchronizing a phonograph record to the picture. Because the talking movie was an instant success, every studio caught on to the potential for this new technology. Unfortunately for De Forest, Western Electric sued him over patent rights regarding certain components in the "phonofilm" system, and he was forced to stop promoting it.

Fourth marriage. De Forest married a fourth and final time at the age of 57, wedding a twenty-one-year-old Hollywood starlet following a six-week courtship. His wife, Marie Mosquini, had much more in common with him than had his previous spouses, including a strong interest in the arts and outdoor activities. Marie remained with De Forest until his death in 1961, in Hollywood, at the age of 87.

> ## The Navy and Communication
>
> The Navy's wireless station in Arlington, Virginia, experimentally arranged a series of five hundred triodes, for successive amplification of a signal to a strength powerful enough to be heard in Paris, France, and Honolulu, Hawaii. This was an incredible feat for the time, 1915. The following year, De Forest broadcast the presidential race between Woodrow Wilson and Charles Evans Hughes, and thousands of people with receivers within a 200 mile radius of his laboratory in the Bronx, New York, were the first in the country to know that Wilson had won the election.

For More Information

Heyn, Ernest V. *Fire of Genius: Inventors of the Past Century.* New York: Anchor Press/Doubleday, 1976.

Levine, I. E. *Electronics Pioneer: Lee De Forest.* New York: Julian Messner, 1964.

Lewis, Thomas S. *Empire of the Air: The Men Who Made Radio.* New York: HarperCollins, 1991.

Vladimir Zworykin

1889-1982

Personal Background

Father unhappy with physics. Born in Russia in 1889, Vladimir Kosma Zworykin was the youngest of seven children. His father, a prominent industrialist in the town of Mourom, ran a shipping line on the Oka River. He hoped his children would also be interested in shipping, banking, and commerce and pursue one of these lucrative fields. But at an early age, his youngest child displayed a rare gift that was hard to ignore. Vladimir was so interested in science that he would stay after school to help his teachers in the science laboratory.

At the age of nine, Vladimir began spending his summers as an apprentice on his father's boats. He was fascinated by electricity and quickly learned how to repair anything electrical.

Upon graduating from high school, Vladimir enrolled in the University of St. Petersburg, where he heard his first physics lecture. On the spot, he decided that he wanted to be a physicist. (Physics is a science that explores the physical properties and composition of objects and the forces that affect them.) His father, who wanted him to become an engineer, was furious at the news. Russia was booming with new industry, and anyone with engineering abilities could go far. An education in physics, he thought, was not practical. Thus, he made Vladimir transfer to the Imperial

▲ Vladimir Zworykin

Event: Developing television.

Role: As a research scientist for the Westinghouse and RCA corporations, Vladimir Zworykin was a pioneer in the development of television, electron microscopy, and infrared vision.

Institute of Technology in St. Petersburg, a move that he hoped would steer his son in the direction of engineering.

Student riots. Zworykin found himself caught in the middle of student riots during his first few weeks of school. Police were called in and he, along with other students, barricaded themselves in one of the campus buildings, where they remained for three days before "surrendering" to authorities. The experience, Zworykin later recalled, was a common one for college students at that point in Russia's history. (Russia was on the eve of a revolution that would see the removal of the ruling czar and an installation of the communist government of Lenin.)

The race for television. Newly emerging theories about the atom (atoms are the tiny particles of which all things are composed; the core of an atom is called the nucleus), coupled with developments in X-rays and radioactivity (the emission of energy from a substance, caused by the spontaneous disintegration of certain unstable nuclei) preoccupied physics students and faculty members at the Imperial Institute of Technology. These new staples of physics provided many opportunities. Zworykin's physics professor, Boris Rosing, was in charge of laboratory projects at the Imperial Institute. Using a cathode ray receiver, he was working on one of the most intriguing technological possibilities of the century—television.

Nipkow's Mechanical TV

Light travels in straight lines in every direction. A television system that did not control which beam of light sent the electric signal would result in light from all parts of a picture striking all parts of the television screen—and a blurry or nonexistent picture. Nipkow inserted a metal disk between the light source and the electronic tube that would convert light to electricity. The disk was punctured with a spiral of small holes. Spinning very rapidly, the disk would scan a whole picture but allow light from only one part of the picture to strike the electronic tube at a time. A complete rotation of the disk would paint a whole picture as the variations in the intensity of light were changed to variations in intensity of electric signals.

Though a practical television system would not exist for decades, the *idea* of television, the transmission of moving pictures, was the obvious next step in the development of electronic communications. What the telegraph (an electrical apparatus for sending coded messages) and telephone had done for sound, scientists were now hoping they could do for sight.

Almost thirty years previously, a German inventor named Paul Nipkow had patented the first television—in 1884! The device was a mechanical scanner, which used a spinning disk to convert the televised scene into an electrical current in the transmitter, and another spinning disk to create the picture in the receiver. The system was not light-sensitive enough to be practical, however, owing in part to its use of mechanical instead of electronic components. Rosing chose Zworykin to be his only laboratory assistant in his private research into television. Knowing that an electronic system would give television much greater potential, Rosing hoped his cathode ray tube would replace Nipkow's mechanical receiver.

In 1910 Rosing and Zworykin were able to demonstrate a television system that used Nipkow's mechanical scanner in the transmitter, but a cathode tube in the receiver. Like earlier attempts at television, it was primitive and impractical; but unlike earlier systems, the cathode ray tube was more efficient and lasted longer than old mechanical systems. The process did indeed reveal that a sure and lasting television system could be developed— and gave Zworykin his mission.

Dedication to television. In 1912 Zworykin graduated from the Imperial Institute with honors and a scholarship in electrical engineering. By now, however, he was hopelessly under the spell of television. Because Zworykin believed that a practical system could be developed only with great improvements in the field of electronics, he decided to continue his education in the discipline that would best advance that aim—theoretical physics.

Zworykin enrolled in the College of France in Paris. There he studied under Paul Langevin, a prominent scientist who drafted Zworykin into X-ray research. He spent a couple of years

Definitions

Amplifying tube: an electronic tube arranged so as to increase the strength of an electric current.

Cathode ray tube: a tube in which electrons are speeded up and formed into a beam as they pass through electromagnetic fields.

Electromagnetic tube: any arrangement of electrodes in a vacuum-filled tube that acts on electric or magnetic fields.

Photoelectric cells: an electric tube that varies the flow of electricity according to the amount of light the tube receives.

Receiver: the mechanism that receives a television or radio message.

Scanner: a device for rapidly moving a beam of electrons across a picture or bit of writing and reproducing it.

Transmitter: the sending mechanism of a radio or television system.

studying the properties of X-rays, which were still very poorly understood. Then, while Zworykin was at home for the summer vacation of 1914, World War I broke out.

Private Zworykin. Like every other young man in Russia, Zworykin was immediately drafted into the army. In a few months' time, he was stationed at Grodno fortress, near the Polish border. Grodno did not have a working radio, though Zworykin soon discovered it had all the parts necessary to assemble one. Taking the initiative, he built a transmitter himself and operated it when it was completed.

> ## TV From Scratch
>
> Because their field was still in its infancy, Rosing and Zworykin had to create everything they needed for their research themselves; in essence, they had to build a television from scratch. This required that they become, among other things, proficient glassblowers in order to fashion their own photocells and amplifying tubes.

After a year and a half, Zworykin was transferred to the Officers Radio School, where he became a commissioned officer and began teaching electronics. When the Russian Revolution broke out in 1917, however, he realized that his scientific career would be in danger if he stayed in Russia. With that in mind, he approached American officials about the prospect of immigrating to the United States.

The United States refused Zworykin's first request for a visa, so he spent several months wandering Russia as a deserter, trying to avoid arrest while watching his country fall deeper into civil war. When an Allied expedition (the Allies were Britain, France, and Russia) landed in Archangel in September 1918 to help Russia's northern defense against the Germans, Zworykin pleaded his case to another American diplomatic official. His explanation of how he would one day develop television must have seemed farfetched, but the official admired his sincerity. He was granted a visa.

Zworykin made his way to London, where he was able to board a ship for America. Since he was an officer, he traveled first-class, though he did not have the formal attire that first-class passengers were expected to wear at dinner. Only when the ship was at sea did he realize how out of place he looked—a refugee in first class. Zworykin arrived in New York in 1919 without knowing much English and spent the next ten months getting on his feet in a new country.

▲ Zworykin holding the cathode ray tube he helped invent; the cathode ray tube was more efficient and lasted longer than old mechanical systems.

Westinghouse. In 1920 Zworykin took a job at Westinghouse Research Laboratories in Pittsburgh, Pennsylvania. Immediately, the new employee tried to convince his superiors to let him work on an all-electronic television system. Finding no one at Westinghouse interested, he left the company within a year and

▲ Zworykin in his laboratory in 1926; in 1923 he had demonstrated the iconoscope, an electronic television transmission tube, for Westinghouse executives. Zworykin was politely asked to pursue "more useful projects."

took a job establishing a laboratory for a petroleum company. This employment took him even further away from any prospect of television research, though, and within two years, he was back at Westinghouse. This time, he had a better position that gave him more free time to work on his own pet projects—especially television. Eventually Westinghouse became interested in pursuing his system and gave him funds to develop it.

Participation: Developing Television

Patents. In 1923 Zworykin patented the iconoscope, an electronic television transmission tube, and demonstrated it for Westinghouse executives. Although it did transmit a picture, the image was marred by poor contrast and low definition, and Westinghouse was unimpressed. Zworykin was politely asked to pursue "more useful projects." He did, but in his spare time he continued to work on television.

In 1924 Zworykin became a United States citizen. That year he also patented the kinescope, a receiving tube. Together, the iconoscope and kinescope comprised the world's first all-electronic television system. Although Westinghouse remained uninterested in his results, Zworykin never gave up. Meanwhile, he continued his education, receiving a doctorate in physics from the University of Pittsburgh in 1926.

Radio Corporation of America. In 1929 Zworykin demonstrated his kinescope for a convention of radio engineers. By this time, he had numerous other patents (including one for color television!) and his kinescope was much improved. The demonstration was met with excitement from the radio community, but his most enthusiastic supporter was David Sarnoff, the vice-president and general manager of the Radio Corporation of America (RCA).

Sarnoff immediately recognized the importance of television, and by the end of the year he had hired Zworykin as the director of RCA's Electronic Research Lab in Camden, New Jersey. At RCA Zworykin continued his work in the general field of electron optics (sending visual messages electrically), making several additional advancements in television. In 1931 he and his staff produced an improved camera with enhanced sensitivity. But for the next two decades, Zworykin investigated other technologies as well.

The electron microscope. Among Zworykin's most important areas of research was electron microscopy. The Camden lab produced its first electron microscope in 1939. It was a prototype, as large as the side of a house. Within a year, though, the group had come up with a revised model that stood only six feet tall—small enough and cheap enough for many industrial and medical laboratories to afford, and simple enough that any competent lab technician could operate it.

The electron microscope was a breakthrough for research in many areas; it allowed scientists to clearly see details twenty to fifty times smaller than could be seen with an ordinary optical microscope. Unlike an ordinary microscope, which uses lenses to magnify visible light, an electron microscope shoots a beam of electrons through a series of magnetic coils. The electromagnetic field around the coils accelerates the electrons and forms them into a beam that focuses the electron flow on the subject. The electrical impulse produces an amplified electron flow that forms a picture in a way similar to the way a TV transmitter and receiver work.

Night vision. In 1940 Zworykin was appointed associate director of research at the Camden laboratories, a prestigious position that reflected the continuing value of his work. During World War II, in 1944, the German High Command accused him of inventing a secret device that would allow Allied pilots to see through fog and clouds. When reporters questioned Zworykin about it, he dismissed the rumor as Nazi propaganda. (Propaganda is selected information—true or false—that is promoted with the aim of persuading people to adopt a particular belief, attitude, or course of action.) In fact, he was working on electron image tubes, which allowed infrared "night vision" for the first time. Infrared light cannot be seen, but its waves are so long that they can pass through materials that would block visible light. Before the war was over, Allied soldiers were seeing in the dark with the sniperscope and the snooperscope, two devices that Zworykin had secretly developed for the war effort.

In 1947 Zworykin was made a vice-president of RCA and in 1954 he officially retired. He continued working, however, as a consultant, with the title of honorary vice-president. By this time, American society was undergoing a cultural revolution, brought about in part by Zworykin's inventions.

Impact of the Electron Microscope

The electron microscope had an enormous impact on the scientific community: by 1950 thousands of electron microscopes were in use all over the world, allowing scientists to see things like viruses and germs—anything of interest, in fact, that had previously been too small to see. Today, the electron microscope is an invaluable research tool in nearly every branch of science.

Aftermath

Zworykin continued working well into his seventies. He died the day before his ninety-third birthday, having lived long enough to see the effects of television upon several successive generations. Overall, though, he was disgusted with the poor quality of television programming (available programs) and said so frequently.

Over the years Zworykin had worked on a number of other, more unusual projects, many involving the use of computers; by suggesting that computers and telephones could someday be linked up for quicker data (information) transmission, Zworykin anticipated the Information Superhighway, today's computer-operated system for sending and receiving messages almost instantly from around the world.

For More Information

Those Inventive Americans. Washington, D.C.: National Geographic Society, 1971.

Yost, Edna. *Modern Americans in Science & Technology.* New York: Dodd, Mead, 1962.

Twentieth-Century Revolutions

1894

Lenin begins writings on revolution and Marxism that will eventually fill fifty-five volumes.

1900

Boxer Rebellion reinforces European power in Asia, demonstrates weakness of Ch'ing dynasty.

1895

Sun Yat-sen's first attempt at revolution fails. He flees to Japan.

1905

Bloody Sunday inaugurates first Russian revolution; forces mild reforms on the czar. Lenin writes exposé of rural poverty in Russia. Czar agrees to form a parliament—the Duma. Sun Yat-sen forms the revolutionary United League.

1911

Mexican Revolution ends dictatorship of Porfirio Díaz. Sun Yat-sen elected provisional president of new Chinese Republic.

1934

Lázaro Cárdenas becomes president of Mexico.

1917

Lenin leads communist takeover of Russia. Russia withdraws from World War I.

1914-18

World War I.

TWENTIETH-CENTURY REVOLUTIONS

Time for revolution. In the mid-nineteenth century, the vast lands of China, long closed to foreigners, were opened by force as British and Portuguese traders demanded and received trading ports along the Chinese border, as well as the freedom to trade in China itself. Competition from foreigners had a negative impact on the Chinese economy. This coupled with the influence of foreign social and political ideas resulted in deepening disillusionment with the oppressive rule of the Ch'ing (also spelled Qing) dynasty, which had held China in virtual isolation since 1644.

Similar repression and lack of access to international markets had long been imposed on the Russian people as well. While Russia struggled to modernize its economy, it was dragged into World War I, in which millions of its young men perished. Economic disaster and war weariness made Russia ripe for the overthrow of the czar, head of the ruling Romanov family. Throughout Europe and America, the work of German social theorist Karl Marx—who endorsed a classless, stateless communist society where all would be equal, contributing according to their abilities and receiving according to their needs—gave hope to millions of hungry and suffering peasants.

In North America, meanwhile, Mexico was becoming increasingly intolerant of foreign intrusion. For more than three

▲ **A scene from the Russian Revolution; economic disaster and war weariness made Russia ripe for the overthrow of the czar, head of the ruling family.**

hundred years, Mexico had been exploited by the Europeans, who found two factors to their advantage: rich resources and a large population of native Mexicans who were easily forced into labor. Nineteenth-century expulsion of the French-controlled government had led to one inept regime after another. And the wealthy, primarily the owners of large haciendas (plantations), continued to exploit the region's Indian population. By the dawn of the twentieth century, Mexico, too, was primed for revolution.

Communism. Many champions of change led the way to revolution around the world. Marx dreamed of a society in which each person would work for the good of all. In Russia, Marx's vision was advanced by a bright revolutionary named **Lenin** (born Vladimir Ilyich Ulyanov). For more than seventeen years, Lenin campaigned for the people of Russia to rise up and rid the nation of the dictatorial czarist system that kept many of them in poverty and despair. Eventually he succeeded; the czar was overthrown (and later assassinated along with his family), and Lenin led Russia into a socialist government, for which it was ill-prepared. The result was chaos. Ultimately Lenin's model of communism revealed itself to be as tyrannical and violent as the system it had replaced.

Republicanism. In the South of China, a man educated in the West emerged and began to stir the people to action. When his first efforts at revolt failed, he fled abroad and rallied Chinese overseas to support rebellion against the ancient Ch'ing dynasty. After sixteen years in exile, **Sun Yat-sen** succeeded in getting most of the provinces of China to secede from the Ch'ing government and form a new Republic of China. But China had been under the domination of the Ch'ing so long that no other unifying force existed. The country was effectively divided into North and South. Sun tried in vain to develop unity. Like Lenin, he did not live to see his dreams fulfilled, but left behind a powerful successor who accomplished much of what he had set out to do.

In Mexico, the rule of Maximilian of Austria, a puppet emperor supported by France, was replaced by the dictatorship of Porfirio Díaz in 1876. After Díaz was removed as a result of the Mexican Revolution of 1910, the leaders of many rebellious factions jockeyed for control of the country. A series of administrations grappled with reform and sought to establish a place for Mexico among the industrial nations of the world.

Eventually, the mantle of leadership was passed to **Lázaro Cárdenas,** who had been a general during the revolutionary period and later governor of the southwestern state of Michoacán. Cárdenas remodeled land ownership, improved the educational system, took control of the Mexican oil industry away from foreign interests, and recognized Indian rights, all of which made significant strides toward improved living conditions for the people of Mexico. Still, as was the case with his fellow revolutionaries in China and Russia, Cárdenas left office with his mission incomplete. Most of his accomplishments were ultimately erased by later rulers of Mexico.

Lenin

1870-1924

Personal Background

Early environment. Vladimir Ilyich Ulyanov was born April 10, 1870, in Simbirsk (now Ulyanovsk), Russia on the Volga River, to Maria Alexandrovna Blank, daughter of a surgeon and landowner, and Ilya Nikolaevich Ulyanov. Vladimir's father was a *chinovnik,* or career civil servant, who had worked his way into the lower noble society. At first a teacher, by 1874 he had become a director of public schools. Maria inherited one-fifth of her wealthy father's land, so the Ulyanov family, which included six children (four of whom survived to adulthood), lived comfortably, though not lavishly.

Alexander (Sasha), the oldest son, would have the greatest influence on young Vladimir's life, though the two were very different in temperament. Alexander was quiet and serious; Vladimir, although equally bright, was given to childhood pranks and spent many hours sitting in the large black punishment chair in his father's study. As children, Alexander and Vladimir were good students, as were an older sister, Anna, and the younger children, Maria and Dimitri.

Vladimir's grandfather on his mother's side was a liberal-minded man, but his own father was conservative—never wishing to express an opinion that might endanger his position as a government worker. Nonetheless, all his children would become rev-

▲ Lenin

Event: Leading the Russian Revolution.

Role: Working in exile from Switzerland and England, Lenin encouraged the socialist overthrow of the czarist government of Russia. Then, when a minority group, the Mensheviks, failed to form an effective government, Lenin helped establish a new communist government, which led to the formation of the United Soviet Socialist Republics (U.S.S.R.).

olutionaries. This began when Vladimir's brother Alexander went off to college at the University of St. Petersburg.

At first Alexander was a model student; in 1911 he won a gold medal for his study on annelids (a class that includes worms and leeches). A few months later, though, he pawned the medal to buy dynamite. Around the same time, Alexander became deeply involved in a student movement that planned to assassinate Czar Alexander III of Russia. The police arrested the five would-be terrorists on the street as they transported the bomb to its target. At his trial, Alexander took credit for planning the affair, declaring, "We are allowed to develop our intellectual powers but we are not allowed to use them for the benefit of the people" (Appignanesi, p. 31). On May 8, 1887, Alexander and his comrades were hanged. Vladimir Ulyanov had just turned seventeen.

Vladimir's father had died suddenly in 1886. His mother had sat alone in court in order to see her oldest son once more before his death. When she returned home, she was shunned by her neighbors. Vladimir continued on with his own studies; he, too, was preparing to enter college. But from the moment of Alexander's execution, his life was dedicated to the goals of revolution.

Expulsion from school. Within three months of starting classes at Kazan University, Vladimir, who would later use the single name Lenin, was expelled after an arrest at a student protest meeting; he then joined his mother and sister Anna at the family estate in Kukushkino. His mother hoped to rescue him by making him a gentleman farmer. She gave him 250 acres, and he made a weak attempt at farming. Most of the time, however, Lenin studied and read.

In 1890, as a result of his mother's repeated requests to authorities and his father's respected name, Lenin was allowed to enter the University of St. Petersburg as an "external" student,

Lenin, the Name

Always a revolutionary, Vladimir Ulyanov used many aliases to escape state police wherever he went. Upon his release from a prison term in Siberia, he needed a new alias. Ulyanov and his work were banned in St. Petersburg, the capital of Russia, but he had ideas about publishing an antigovernment newsletter. He would print it outside the country under a new alias—N. Lenin. Over the years he kept this name, sometimes using other initials with the last name.

isolated from the rest of the student body. He completed the four-year law course in less than a year and graduated in 1891 at the top of his class. For a short time he practiced law, serving the poor in Samara.

On his return to St. Petersburg in 1893, Lenin met Nadezhda Krupskaya, who would become his wife. The two had a great deal in common. She came from an upper-class family suddenly made poor when her father was suspended from his job for "liberalism." Both Lenin and Krupskaya were social democrats. When they met at a socialist meeting, he was twenty-four and already balding. She was twenty-six and very beautiful, her strong features slightly resembling his mother's.

Revolutionary. By 1895 Lenin had decided that his life's work would be revolution. He traveled outside the country to meet with older revolutionaries who had been trying for years to engineer the overthrow of the Russia's Romanov family, of which the czar was head. The revolutionaries tutored Lenin in political philosophy, especially the work of the influential social theorist Karl Marx. Marx, whose ideas form the basis of communism, urged the formation of a classless, stateless society where all would be equal, contributing according to their abilities and receiving according to their needs. Lenin then returned to Russia to continue his work in the underground. He soon formed an association, the Struggle for the Liberation of the Working Class, traveled to Moscow, wrote tracts and leaflets, and organized strikes.

Almost a Game
The young revolutionaries relied on secret codes and knocks. Lenin was always inventing ways to strengthen their security. One historian described his early enchantment with such intrigues:

> Lenin was a great practitioner of these devices. He wrote [a letter to a comrade that read]: "You must write in Indian ink. It would be better if you were to add a small crystal of potassium bichromate ($K_2Cr_2O_7$); then it would not wash off. Use *thinner* paper." He continued: "It is essential to use liquid paste; not more than a teaspoonful of starch to a glass of water (and moreover, potato flour, not ordinary flour which is too strong)." His first letter out of prison was directed to his landlady and was written in code. (Moorehead, p. 42)

Prisoner. In December 1895, on the verge of releasing a revolutionary newspaper, Lenin was arrested; a dentist friend had turned informant for the reward. But Lenin was not unhappy in

▲ Lenin making a speech in Moscow's Red Square in May 1919; no change in the government would satisfy him short of disposing of the czar and replacing the czarist dictatorship with one led by the Russian workers.

jail. He adopted an attitude of acceptance and did not attempt to escape, using the time to expand his mind, rationing his day into hours for writing and translation, reading and practicing languages. Nor did he neglect his physical care; he did push-ups several times a day. Exercise was also a way to keep warm in his cell.

Lenin had access to the prison library and books from outside; his mother and sister sent food and warm clothes, and he was even able to smuggle his work beyond the prison walls. After fourteen months, he was sentenced—without trial—to three more years, to be served in Siberia, a vast territory in the remote north-eastern part of Russia infamous for its harsh climate.

Siberia. But even prison in the eastern region was not terribly severe. Prisoners able to pay their own way took a train, reported en route, and set up house on arrival in the village to which they were assigned. There were no guards or gates. Although travel was not allowed without permission, one could move freely within the province to visit neighbors. Prisoners could also marry and take jobs. The immense vastness separating Siberia from the rest of Russia, however, was more isolating than traditional prison walls. Still, for the revolutionaries, isolation proved positive; they were able to think, write, and discuss plans without fear of police. For many, the rigorous climate actually improved health.

Self-education. In February 1897, Lenin departed for Sushenskoye, a community said to be hidden by mosquitoes when not snowed in. There were only two other exiles there. Lenin liked the solitude; he went duck- and snipe-hunting—in his letters home he mentioned the difficulties of getting a good dog—but the majority of his time was spent working. He asked constantly for books: histories, novels, even dictionaries and grammar texts. From these he taught himself English, German, Italian, and French. In 1898 Nadezhda was arrested; she was allowed to join Lenin on the condition that they marry. She arrived in May of that year, ill and exhausted, to find Lenin plump and tanned.

Participation: Leading the Russian Revolution

Rebel in exile. By 1900 Lenin and Nadezhda were permitted to leave Siberia. He and other leaders of the anti-czar movement made plans to distribute *Iskra* ("The Spark"), a journal intended to "fire up" Marxist supporters. After his prison term, however, he and his friends were constantly watched. Lenin was forced to move often.

Lenin devoted himself to the newspaper—traveling the country during the spring and summer to make preparation for its distribution. It was still illegal for him to be in the nation's capital, St. Petersburg. When he was caught there, he again spent a few days in jail. Still, he managed to be in Geneva, Switzerland, by July. For the next decade or so, Lenin would direct his plans to overthrow the czar mostly from outside of Russia.

Lenin was uncompromising in pursuit of his revolutionary goals; no change in the government would satisfy him short of disposing of the czar and replacing the czarist dictatorship with one led by the Russian workers. Other rebel leaders, including Leon Trotsky, Lenin's close friend, often disagreed with his writings. These writings were, of course, banned in Russia. Indeed, the December 1900 debut issue of *Iskra* was confiscated by border police. Later editions, wrapped in waterproof bundles, were delivered to drop-off sites on the Baltic and Black Seas by merchant ships, or sent through Austria, Persia, or Egypt. Most managed to enter Russia, where they encouraged revolutionary fervor.

For seventeen years, Lenin and his wife remained on the move, lodging in back rooms from Munich, Germany, to Zurich, Switzerland to London, England.

Planning for dictatorship. Lenin knew the Social Democratic Congress in Brussels would be an important event for the party. On July 30, 1903, sixty delegates assembled in the heat of a flour warehouse draped in red. It was supposed to be a "secret meeting," but the ensuing shouts and loud arguments, audible outside, quickly attracted attention. Within a week the Belgian police ordered the delegates to leave. The entire group then departed for London.

At the core of the conflict was whether the party should be a democracy or controlled by a central committee. Lenin favored the latter; he wanted *Iskra* to control the committee, and he would continue to direct *Iskra*. The delegates fought among themselves continually. They gave up on August 23, declaring the convention a disaster.

Lenin's Writings

Over the years, Lenin wrote many books and articles encouraging the revolt of citizens in capitalist countries (where private interests, instead of the government, control production and distribution of goods in a system characterized by competition in a free market). Among the earliest was a pamphlet titled "What Are the 'Friends of the People' and How Do They Fight Against the Social Democrats." Since these pamphlets were first composed in yellow notebooks, they came to be known as the "Little Yellow Books" and were accepted as the manifesto, or guidelines, for Russian communism.

But by 1904 Lenin was active again, so obsessed with regaining power from the Mensheviks (a powerful minority group within the Social Democratic Workers' Party; Lenin was leader of the majority Bolsheviks) that he paid scant attention to the Russo-Japanese War. He published *Vperyed* ("Forward"), and new forces rallied around "the old man."

In early 1905, a Russian Orthodox priest named Father Gapon led two hundred thousand workers from St. Petersburg to the czar's winter palace to demonstrate for better working conditions. On January 9 government troops fired into the crowd, killing a thousand protesters. In 112 industrial towns and on ten rail lines, activity stopped completely when workers protested with a general strike, the largest in labor history. Eventually, in this first of two Russian revolutions, the czar was forced to yield some of his power and establish an advisory council, the Duma. It was soon apparent, however, that the Duma would have little voice in government, and so the turmoil within Russian society grew. The country was also faced with dire economic problems and the onset of World War I.

Lenin's cause was aided by this war. In 1917, with fighting fronts on both sides, Germany sought a way to defeat the Russians quickly, which would enable its military to direct full attention to the other front, in Belgium and France. By then living in Germany, Lenin was encouraged to impress communist ideas strongly on Russian workers, soldiers, and sailors. The plan was effective, with weary Russian soldiers neglecting their orders and forming "soviets," mini-congresses in which groups of soldiers would sit down in the midst of battle to debate whether or not to obey their officers.

Revolutionary sentiment grew so great among the Russian forces that Russia had no choice but to withdraw from the war. By 1917 the czar—who was later assassinated along with his wife and children—had been forced to abdicate and a temporary government was established. (The leader of this government, Alexander Kerensky, was almost immediately unpopular because of his desire to continue Russian participation in World War I which had already cost the country millions of soldiers.)

▲ The main street of Petrograd, Russia, in March 1917, as revolutionaries turned their machine guns on an angry crowd. During three years of civil war, Lenin embarked on a program of violence that would continue for the rest of his life.

Dictator of Russia. Lenin soon felt that his opportunity to take control of Russia had arrived. Again the Germans supported his actions, providing him safe passage to the Russian border. Lenin rallied his supporters and was able to successfully take over the Russian government. His rule was not without resistance, however. Most Russians feared Germany and were not happy that it had helped Lenin take control. Three years of civil war ensued, during which Lenin embarked on a program of violence that would continue for the rest of his life and into the regime of his

▲ Lenin (center left) next to a saluting Leon Trotsky, reviewing a parade in Moscow's Red Square in 1919; one of Lenin's first acts as head of state had been to assign Trotsky the task of building up a "red," or communist, army.

successor, Josef Stalin, whose reputation for brutality eventually exceeded Lenin's.

In one incident, twelve thousand sailors who were gathered in a single port decided to strike for better working conditions and pay. One of Lenin's first acts as communist dictator had been to assign his old friend Leon Trotsky the task of building up a "red," or communist, army. Trotsky had been very effective and was directed to put down the sailor strike. Then, without warning, but within the instructions given by Trotsky, Lenin's Red Army began shelling the seaport. Sailors and soldiers fought house to house, with the underarmed sailors gradually losing. Finally, some escaped to Sweden, but most sailors and many soldiers were killed in the fighting. A few were taken prisoner; Lenin then ordered their execution by firing squad.

Such action helped Lenin shape the communist Union of Soviet Socialist Republics (U.S.S.R.), the realization of his Marxist model. All farms and factories were controlled by the central government—supposedly to be operated, managed, and profited from by the people who worked them. In practice, though, this was not always the case.

Aftermath

The emergence of Stalin. By 1924 Lenin, still plagued by dissension in Russia and with much larger economic problems than he had faced on his ascent to power, had begun to have second thoughts about Marxism. He began to feel that he had moved too quickly and that the Russian people were not yet ready for socialism.

That year Lenin suffered a series of strokes that took him away from government periodically and finally took his life. Josef Stalin was a member of the governing soviet (collective) and had proven a very diligent worker. Lenin, who really cared little for the actual work of governing, had been happy to let Stalin take first one job and then another until he had assumed a very large role in the new government.

On Lenin's death, this advantage allowed Stalin to push Trotsky aside and take control of the U.S.S.R. He immediately began a series of purges that eliminated thousands of possible opponents to his rule. These purges persisted until Stalin died in 1953. Trotsky was exiled from Russia in 1929, but because Stalin continued to perceive him as a threat, he was tracked down in Mexico and executed in 1940.

For More Information

Appignanesi, Robert, and Oscar Zanate. *Lenin for Beginners.* New York: Pantheon Books, 1978.

Kaiser, Robert G. *Russia: The People and the Power—Fully Updated.* New York: Washington Square, 1984.

Moorehead, Alan. *The Russian Revolution.* New York: Carroll and Graf, 1987.

Trotsky, Leon. *The Young Lenin.* Translated by Max Eastman. Garden City, New York: Doubleday, 1972.

Sun Yat-sen

1866-1925

Personal Background

Early environment. Sun Yat-sen was born Sun Wen on November 12, 1866, in the village of Choyhung, or Blue Thriving Village, near China's West River. His father, Sun Tao-chuan, owned a small farm prosperous enough to keep six children well fed and schooled. He traced his ancestry to a duke from the north who had settled locally after the fall of the Ming dynasty in 1644. (A dynasty is a powerful family that maintains its ruling position for a considerable time.)

Sun Yat-sen was the youngest son; his father was in his fifties when he was born. Later in his life, Sun would describe his childhood as "an unbelievably happy period in a life of continual strain."

Sun was influenced early on by his uncle, who had fought in the Taiping Rebellion (a peasant uprising that lasted from 1851 to 1864 and seriously weakened the ruling dynasty) and whom Sun idolized. He was also exposed to the lifestyle of Chinese who had lived overseas and who would later become his strongest source of support. To bring the Western world (primarily the industrially advanced countries of North America and Europe) into China, they made clear, was the only way to modernize and move ahead.

Two widowed aunts also lived with Sun's family. Because their husbands had died in California, the family swore no sons

▲ Sun Yat-sen

Event: Moving China from dynastic rule to democracy.

Role: Sun Yat-sen served as the voice of the Chinese Revolution of 1911. He worked tirelessly throughout his life, both from within China and abroad, to overthrow the Ch'ing dynasty and establish a democracy. Though he would see the birth of a republic in China, he would not live to preside over a united China.

would go overseas. Nonetheless, when Sun was six, his brother Ah Mei, twelve years his senior, left home for Hawaii. There, Ah Mei prospered farming the rich lowland soil. He returned in 1877 to take a wife, rebuild his parent's house, and describe the riches of the islands. Sun begged his father to send him to Hawaii, but he refused. Sun persisted. Two years later, with his father's approval, he sailed to Honolulu on a British ship.

Sun worked in his brother's general store and entered the church-supported Iolani College in 1879. He proved to be a good student and quickly converted to Anglican Christianity, undergoing baptism. When he admitted he had become a Christian, Ah Mei wrote home about his brother's disrespect for custom. By this time, Sun was eighteen—old enough to marry. Ah Mei sent him home to find a bride.

Sun returned home to discover that he was no longer content with village life, particularly the rituals associated with it. He even tore apart idols during a local festival; only the people's esteem for his father saved him from death. Instead, he was banished. He headed for Hong Kong with only letters of recommendation; he entered Queen's College in the mid-1880s bent on studying medicine and married a local girl while still in school.

To complete his medical studies, Sun interned at Pok Tsai Hospital in Canton and then spent the next several years at Alice Memorial Hospital in Hong Kong. In 1892 Sun Yat-sen moved to Macao to practice medicine. Macao was a Portuguese territory in southeast China. Officials there refused to allow Sun to practice, since he lacked proper Portuguese credentials.

Sun worked instead in Guangzhou, where he met people who, like his uncle, had fought against the Ch'ing regime. (The Ch'ing [also spelled Qing] dynasty was set up by the Manchu people, who conquered China and had governed it since 1644.) Sun decided that overthrowing the ancient dynasty was a necessity for China. In 1894 he returned to Honolulu and started a revolutionary society called X'ing Zhong Hui, the Society for the Revival of China. The next year, Sun set up headquarters for the organization in Hong Kong. He had become a professional revolutionary. At the time he wrote, "All the years between 1885 and 1895 were

▲ After his 1895 attempt to seize the government offices in Guangzhou failed, Sun waged a personal rebellion; he cut off his queue, donned Western clothing, and grew a mustache (which also served as a disguise).

like one day in my hard fight for national liberty, and my medical practice was no more to me than a means to introduce my propaganda to the world" (Sun in Chen, p. 25).

123

Participation: Moving China From Dynastic Rule to Democracy

Trials and errors. In 1895 Sun attempted to seize the government offices in Guangzhou; the plot was discovered and this first step in armed revolution ended in failure. Sun escaped to Japan, but forty-six others were executed. In Japan, Sun waged a personal rebellion; he cut off his queue (a traditional long braid), donned Western clothing, and grew a mustache. He was now a wanted man, watched by representatives of the Ch'ing government. His new look served as a disguise. To further protect himself, he moved frequently and used a different alias in every city. Sun traveled extensively, trying to coordinate financial and political backing for the revolutionary cause among Chinese living overseas. He spoke in southern China, Hawaii, and Japan and later made lecture tours of the United States and Europe.

Apprehended in England. In London in October 1896, Sun encountered one of his old instructors, James Cantlie. After visiting his friend at home, Sun was returning to his lodging in a nearby hotel when he was suddenly and forcibly escorted to the Chinese embassy. He was locked in a room at the top of the building and told he was going to be deported to China, where he would be executed.

Sun dropped messages out the window of his makeshift cell, hoping to somehow get word to Cantlie. He was finally able to persuade one of his captors to deliver a note. Cantlie went immediately to the local police, who informed him that the matter was beyond their jurisdiction; he tried Scotland Yard (headquarters of the Criminal Investigation Department of the London Metropolitan Police) and the *London Times,* but no one would listen to him.

Sun's Faith

In his account *Kidnapped in London,* Sun described his feelings of hopelessness after his arrest:

My despair was complete, and only by prayers to God could I gain comfort. Still the dreary days and still more dreary nights wore on, and but for the comfort afforded me by prayer I believe I should have gone mad. After my release I related to Dr. Cantlie how prayer was my one hope, and told him how I should never forget the feeling that seemed to take possession of me as I rose from my knees on the morning of Friday, October 16th, a feeling of calmness, hopefulness, and confidence, that assured me my prayer was heard, and filled me with hope that all would be well. (Sun in Chen, p. 42)

國民　　　　華中

1911 ANNIVERSARY REPUBLIC OF CHINA 1961

UNITED STATES POSTAGE

4¢

SUN YAT-SEN

▲ A U.S. postage stamp commemorating the fiftieth anniversary of the founding of the republic of China. Sun Yat-sen worked tirelessly throughout his life to overthrow the Ch'ing dynasty and establish a democracy.

Finally, a reporter from the *Globe* took interest. The public's response on reading the *Globe* headlines forced Sun's release on October 24. At age thirty, Sun Yat-sen was suddenly an international celebrity, seen by many in the West as the leader of the Chinese cause.

The Boxer Rebellion

The Boxer Rebellion of 1900 was a violent uprising in China directed at foreigners. Supported by the ruling Ch'ing dynasty, a secret society called the "Harmonious Fists"—"boxers" to the Europeans—opposed European influence and commercial exploitation in China. They attacked missionaries and Chinese converts to Christianity. An attempt by the European powers to protect their citizens in China with troops was defeated. The German minister in Peking was killed and foreign missions throughout the country were harassed for two months, until an international force intervened and stopped the rebellion. In 1901 China was forced to sign the Boxer Protocol, which required that it provide extensive compensation to the foreign powers that had been affected by the violence.

Sun continued to work outside the country to mobilize young Chinese. Meanwhile, rebels inside the country were having only minimal success. In 1905 Sun founded the Tong Meng Hui, or United League, and began setting up overseas offices in Japan. The league published a newspaper called the *People's Journal;* it was the voice of the new movement. The *Journal* carried an early draft of Sun's "People's Principles," his plans for a Chinese democracy, in 1907. In addition, between 1906 and 1908 the Tong Meng Hui led small uprisings in the countryside; Sun personally participated in one in Guangxi province. All attempts, however, failed to overthrow the Ch'ing.

Destabilization in China. Still, the political situation in China was changing as the Ch'ing faced challenges on several fronts. Armed conflicts with Britain, Russia, and Japan were disastrous. And for a quarter of a century, the aging dynasty had been vulnerable to exploitation by the West, which resulted in unfavorable economic competition. The Boxer Rebellion of 1900 had been the Ch'ing's last failure to rid itself of foreign power; the presence of the West was still strong.

Indeed, to many European nations, as well as the United States, China seemed a wealth of resources, from cheap labor to new industries. Reaching this wealth would require cross-country transportation. So the Western nations had supported the building of railroads in China, which deepened penetration of the Chinese interior by foreigners.

Revolution. In fact, it was a railroad that touched off the revolution that Sun had so far been unable to produce. The populous and prosperous Sichuan province, along with the city of Wuhan in Hubei, had sold shares as a sort of forced tax to finance the railroad's construction. The newest railroad was, therefore, a provincial, or state, affair, but the Ch'ing wanted it as an imperial property (belonging to the emperor). In May 1911, the government obtained a loan from the West, took over construction, and "nationalized" the railroad.

Sun's goal for China was to modernize it—to Westernize the nation's industry. But he and his supporters also recognized the importance of provincial efforts. To them this takeover of the railroad was outrageous—another example of European-supported Manchu domination. A series of skirmishes began with the local militia. On October 9, 1911, a bomb exploded in militia headquarters in Wuhan; the Ch'ing retaliated with mass beheadings and imprisonments. But some government troops joined forces with the rebels and took Wuhan. Then, on October 22, Hubei declared its independence from the capital of Peking. One by one the major cities and provinces declared their independence from the Ch'ing government. By the end of November, fifteen of the eighteen Chinese provinces had seceded.

President of the republic. In 1911 Sun was named provisional president of the New Republic of China. Nonetheless, he took control of a divided nation. He had worked to overthrow the Ch'ing from bases near Canton, in the South, but needed the powerful army of the North to complete the conquest. That army was led by Yuan Shikai. Together, Sun and Yuan had succeeded in ousting the Ch'ing, but once the imperial government was defeated, they remained the respective heads of two different factions. Sun Yat-sen had dedicated his life to establishing a unified Chinese republic; now there was a strong possibility that the country would remain divided.

To avoid this, Sun gave up the post of provisional president, relinquishing it to Yuan Shikai, whose military expertise was crucial to preventing civil war and keeping the nation unified. Yuan took office in 1912 and immediately revealed his disdain for the republic—instead he hoped to make himself the new emperor and effectively set out to create another dictatorship. In 1915 he declared himself "President for Life."

When Yuan dissolved the new parliament of China, Sun left the government and fled to Japan. From exile, he continued to try to influence the political direction of China, concentrating on his southern strongholds. His efforts helped foster a rebellion against the Yuan government in 1913 and wholesale revolt of the southern provinces in 1915 and 1916. In the summer of 1916, Yuan died, and Sun Yat-sen returned to Canton, where he planned to establish a new Chinese republic in the South and eventually expand it to include all of China. The country was still strongly divided, however, and Sun would not live to see his goal accomplished.

Aftermath

Last Words. Sun continued his attempts to consolidate power until he was weakened by cancer in 1925. No treatment was effective in combating the disease. Sun was moved to a colleague's country home. He was visited by several of his key followers, who implored him for a final statement. They reportedly had followed Sun for many years. Surely, if Sun would leave them a message, it would serve as a guide for national life. On March 11, Sun responded in a telegram:

> I thought I would come here and further our national unity and peace. I proposed to convoke the People's Convention and to put into practice my Three Principles of the People and the Five-power Constitution for the reconstruction of a new China; but I have been seized with a stupid disease and now I am past all cure. Really, to live and die makes no difference to me personally, but to leave unrealised the principles I struggled for so many years grieves me deeply. Strive for the early convocation of the People's Convention and try to realise the Three Principles of the People and the Five-power Constitution. If you do this, I shall "close my eyes after my death." (Sun in Chen, pp. 219-20)

Despite doctor's orders to stay silent and sleep, Sun prepared for a conference with the northern leaders to be held in

Peking. Thus Sun died with his power on the rise and the hope of a united China shining brightly. It is said that he whispered with his last breath, "Ho... Ho... Ping, fan-dao, chiu... chiu... chung-kuo" ("Peace ... struggle... save China"; Sun in Chen, p. 220).

In 1927, two years after Sun's death, his supporter and colleague Chiang Kai-shek succeeded in uniting China and forming a new republic. In 1949, however, Chiang would lose the epic struggle for political control of China, his former ally Mao Zedong (also spelled Mao Tse-tung) wresting power from him. Since then, Maoist communism has been the system of government in China.

For More Information

Bloodworth, Dennis. *The Chinese Looking Glass*. New York: Farrar, Straus,1980.

Chen, Stephen, and Robert Payne. *Sun Yat-sen: A Portrait*. New York: John Day, 1946.

Huntington, Madge. *A Traveler's Guide to Chinese History*. New York: Henry Holt and Company, 1986.

Latourette, Kenneth Scott. *The Chinese: Their History and Culture*. New York: Macmillan, 1934.

Seagrave, Sterling. *Dragon Lady: The Life and Legend of the Dowager Empress of China*. New York: Alfred A. Knopf, 1992.

Lázaro Cárdenas

1895-1970

Personal Background

Early environment. The Cárdenas family lived in Jiquilpan, a mile-high town near Lake Chapala in southwest Mexico. The town was know for its *rebozos* (shawls), and some of Cárdenas's ancestors were weavers. The majority of the family, however, were sharecroppers who scraped a living from tiny farms controlled by the nearby Guaracha hacienda (plantation).

Cárdenas's father, Damasco, had owned a small store in town, but by the time he was ready to marry, he had joined a relative operating a soap factory; he then opened a billiard hall, Reunion of Friends, with a single table. None of these ventures, however, earned much money—neither did his practice of folk medicine. So when Damasco married Felicitas del Rio, a member of a devout Catholic farming family, she added to the family finances by sewing.

Thanks to Felicitas's godmother, the young couple lived in a comfortable house on the town's main street. The house even had its own well in the patio. Lázaro Cárdenas del Rio was born in this home on March 25, 1895. Lázaro was a *mestizo*—of mixed Spanish and Tarascan Indian heritage.

Jiquilpan was an unusual town in that it had two schools, one for boys and one for girls. Cárdenas attended the school for boys

▲ **Lázaro Cárdenas**

Event: Reforming Mexico.

Role: Lázaro Cárdenas led rebel troops against Mexican dictator Victoriano Huerta during the Mexican Revolution, later becoming a general in the Mexican army. After he was elected president of Mexico, Cárdenas instituted massive land reforms and public works projects while also establishing Mexico's place in international economics. He is considered the most popular president in his country's history.

through the sixth grade. The school had only one teacher for the 150 boys, but he managed to provide his students with a sound education and instill pride in their country, telling stories of the battles of Mexican heroes José Morelos and Benito Juarez against the French and the oppression of the Catholic Church. Shy and quiet, Cárdenas kept mainly to himself at school; classmates nicknamed him the "Sphinx of Jiquilpan." (A sphinx is a mysterious person, as well as a creature from Greek mythology.)

Cárdenas preferred talking to the old men in the town square or to his father's friends, who lent him books and lectured him on history and botany. The schoolboy worked on his grandfather's farm during vacations from school. When he finished at the local school, the family faced a dilemma: should Cárdenas go away to school in a larger town? Or should he go to work? Although not religious himself, Cárdenas's father had thought that perhaps his son would go into the ministry, but at that time, it seemed better for him to get a job.

Cárdenas took a position in the tax collector's office. From that vantage point, he watched with disapproval as federal agents overrode local authorities for their own benefit. Cárdenas saw corruption in the government even more clearly when he became assistant to the secretary of the regional political boss. Mexico had, by then, endured twenty-five years of dictatorial government by Porfirio Díaz.

Revolution. When, in 1911—the year that Cárdenas's father died—Francesco Madero overthrew the "dictatorship" of Díaz and promised a more democratic government, Cárdenas joined most other Mexicans in renewed hope for reform. Díaz had led Mexico to higher standing as a nation and to better international marketing of its exports. He had, however, done this by exploiting the native peoples of Mexico. When asked about his improvement of Mexican finances, Díaz had said, "God gives the resources, and the Indian does the work" (Townsend, p. 29).

It was hoped by many that Madero would reform land ownership, abolishing the hacienda system that had concentrated good land in the hands of a few powerful owners. That hope, however, was short-lived. Madero was soon assassinated and replaced by

Victoriano Huerta. Despite his ancestry—Huerta was a full-blooded Indian—he quickly showed that he would become an even more stern dictator than Díaz had been. It was not long before a revolution broke out to unseat Huerta and restore democracy. Men like Pancho Villa and Emiliano Zapata and groups such as the Yaqui Indians led the fight.

Soldier. By this time, Cárdenas had begun to add to the family income by working part-time in a print shop. He joined the revolution by printing posters and pamphlets opposing the government. When one of these was carelessly left out where government officials could see it, Cárdenas was forced into greater action.

Cárdenas had received some military training as a thirteen-year-old, when one of Díaz's generals had organized a militia in Jiquilpan. Now he joined the fighting against government forces. Beginning as the leader of a few rebels, he rose to the rank of captain under such leaders as Alvaro Obregón and Plutarco Calles. Often defeated by superior forces, Cárdenas nonetheless proved a fearless soldier.

Once Cárdenas joined a small group preparing to ambush federal troops. While others hid behind rock fences, he knelt, gun-in-hand, in the middle of the road to await the enemy. Fortunately, the first travelers on the road were friendly peasant farmers driving their mules. The incident illustrates the sometimes foolhardy courage of Cárdenas. By the time Obregón and Pedro Carranza overthrew President Huerta, Cárdenas had risen to the rank of general, despite Obregón's opinion that he was trustworthy but incompetent.

Military commander. After the revolution, Cárdenas longed to settle into a political position and help hasten the fulfillment of the Mexican peasants' dreams of land reform. First, a constitution had to be drawn up and approved and a stable government established. The leaders of the revolution encouraged Cárdenas to remain a military commander. He was stationed in Tampico. This stay in Tampico would later prove useful, since it gave Cárdenas an opportunity to view Mexico's blossoming petroleum industry firsthand. Meanwhile, the nation's leaders jockeyed for the presidency, facing the near-chaos that resulted partly from divided leadership in the revolution.

Participation: Reforming Mexico

Governor. In 1928 Cárdenas got an opportunity to serve in politics: he was elected governor of Michoacan, his home state. There he began to display the leadership skills and direction he would take when he was later elected president of Mexico.

Cárdenas found that, despite the revolution, nothing had changed in Michoacan; the old hacienda owners still controlled the land, and the wealthy clergy still suppressed reform. Together, these groups wielded power over the masses of peasants. To counteract their authority, Cárdenas began to organize peasant farm workers and unite them with college students, teachers, and liberal civil servants to form the Confederation Regional Michoacana del Trabajo (Michoacan Confederation of Workers). By 1932 this organization was a powerful political force of more than a hundred thousand members. Cárdenas also helped organize women into a Feminist Federation, which concerned itself mostly with such issues as temperance (abstinence from liquor), though the governor did help them train to become fighters in case of an emergency.

Cárdenas's period as governor also revealed that he would never forget his heritage. He walked and talked with the peasants, attended dinners and parties in their humble homes, willing to listen to their problems at any time. Cárdenas said that the peasants had so little that the least he could do was to give them his patience. It was not uncommon for the governor to be seen leaning against a doorway or fence, listening to the cares of passersby. In this way, Cárdenas established himself as a man

---

Cárdenas in Politics

One historian described Cárdenas's trying to achieve political significance in this way:

> When necessary, he bent with the wind, looked the other way when his colleagues dipped into the public coffer, and never questioned the wisdom of his superiors. Knowing intimately the jungle of Mexican politics, he kept his guard up and spoke only when spoken to. The people who knew him say he was *desconfiado*, wary and distrustful, a man who wanted to control his own decisions. (Ruiz, p. 389)

▲ Cárdenas established himself as a man of the people; it was not uncommon for the governor to be seen leaning against a doorway or fence, listening to the cares of passersby.

of the people. He managed Michoacan without resorting to illegalities, while at the same time maintaining his political friendships.

After the revolution, a single powerful political party, the National Revolutionary Party (PNR), dominated politics in Mexico. Cárdenas had become a member of the party, and in 1934 he was ready to contend for the presidency. Another party member, Perez Trevino, also wanted the post, but Cárdenas's reputation as a reform governor made him a favorite with the people. When then-president Plutarco Calles realized this, he endorsed Cárdenas, throwing him the weight of the PNR. Still, Cárdenas felt it

135

was his duty to keep in touch with the people and campaigned as if his competition was a serious challenge. Cárdenas won the election, and the PNR continued to hold sway over Mexican politics for the next sixty years. (The PNR is now known as the PRI, the Institutional Revolutionary Party, and in the mid-1990s still controlled Mexican politics.)

President of Mexico. Cárdenas took office at a time when Mexican workers were gaining confidence and threatening to strike in order to achieve greater rights. Former president Calles thought that the PNR should exert its power to suppress the workers. Cárdenas refused, but he could not control government mandates against striking and owner lockouts of workers from their workplaces. Cárdenas's hands were largely tied because Calles and the PNR had chosen his cabinet for him. Instead of heeding Calles's directions, which were delivered by this cabinet, Cárdenas fired the cabinet and appointed his own.

Rather than punish striking workers, Cárdenas took a train to the northern manufacturing areas to negotiate with bosses who, he felt, were tired of the social struggle and should give up their factories to the workers or the government. Calles objected to these moves, but Cárdenas persisted. Eventually Calles announced his retirement from politics. Cárdenas was then free to begin his own reforms without interference.

Land reform. Cárdenas's first goal was to renew the land reform that had begun after the 1917 constitution was instituted. His idea was to take land from the large landowners and put it in the care of towns and villages. The people in these communities would then decide how to apportion the common lands (*ejidos*) to the workers. The first step was the 1934 Codio Agrario (Agrarian Code), which gave peasants the right to petition government for hacienda lands they had worked. The own-

---

Cárdenas as Candidate and President-elect

During his presidential campaign, Cárdenas traveled more than 27,500 kilometers, 475 of them on horseback. His journeys took him to cities and towns, as well as countless villages off the beaten path—on occasion to pueblos where residents spoke only regional Indian languages, not a word of Spanish. In his acceptance speech after the election, he suggested what was coming in the arena of Mexican politics: "I have been elected president and I intend to be president" (Cárdenas in Ruiz, p. 392). He knew that the leaders of the party would try to control the presidency.

▲ Cárdenas and members of his cabinet, 1938; when Cárdenas was first elected president, Plutarco Calles had chosen his cabinet for him. Instead of heeding Calles's directions, Cárdenas fired the cabinet and appointed his own.

ers were to be paid for this land by the government. The next year Cárdenas instituted a national bank to help with the land transfers.

Cárdenas began his mission in Laguna, a hot region through which two rivers passed and where large foreign conglomerates controlled cotton growth. He broke the land into *ejidos*. The national bank helped provide the *ejidos* with seed and machinery. Profits from the crops would go directly to the peasant farmers. Next came the state of Yucatan, where 272 *ejidos* were created in the largest land reform yet. By 1940 the Cárdenas government had distributed farmland to 1.5 million families.

To further his efforts, Cárdenas began to improve the Mexican educational system, which had decayed since Díaz's efforts to raise educational standards. The schools were used as platforms for social reform.

Business and industry. Cárdenas was committed to bringing Mexico into the world market. He sponsored the construction of roads and railroads to attract foreign capital and worked with Mexican manufacturers to bring their factories up to world standards. One of Mexico's greatest assets was petroleum. The industry was almost totally controlled by foreign interests. Cárdenas encouraged Mexican oil workers to organize.

The resulting 1,800-member union asked the foreign owners to improve their status by providing sixty-five million pesos in benefits and salaries. The foreign owners refused, offering only fourteen million pesos. Cárdenas's government recommended a counter offer of twenty-six million; that, too, was refused. On March 18, 1938, the Cárdenas government took over the petroleum industry. Foreign owners threatened Cárdenas. He responded by threatening to blow up the oil fields if foreign troops entered Mexican territory. Petroleum interests remained in the hands of Mexican workers.

Native Son

Cárdenas never forgot his mestizo (mixed European and Native American) heritage. In 1936 he established the Mexican Department of Indian Affairs (DIA). This differed greatly from the one established in the United States; its purpose was not to set Indians apart in a reservation program, but to provide education and industry to bring Mexico's Indians into mainstream Mexican society. The first action of the DIA was to sponsor eight Indian congresses. Cárdenas attended each congress, listened to the concerns of individual Indian groups, and began a program to solve their problems.

Aftermath

Post-presidency. Under Mexican law, Cárdenas could not run for reelection. He vowed not to behave as his forerunners had and try to control the elections and government after his presidency. When asked how he hoped to avoid such interference, he told reporters that he would have any friends who tried to persuade him otherwise put in jail—he would only talk to his political allies if they confined themselves to discussions of Peruvian Indians rather than Mexican Indians.

In 1940, as Cárdenas was leaving office, Mexico was beginning to show signs of instability in the petroleum industry, and members of the military were beginning to rebel against his reforms. But Cárdenas kept his word, leaving politics when his presidency was over. Later administrations would reverse his reforms and erase most of his accomplishments. For example, in 1936 Cárdenas had given 750 hectares of land to the Yaqui Indians and recognized their independent status and self-rule. President Miguel Alemán Valdés, who held office from 1946 to 1952, dammed the river that watered this land, reducing the Yaqui to poverty, effectively destroying their autonomy and robbing them of their dignity.

Thirty years after Cárdenas had given the Yaqui communal lands, a local chief asked him if the situation then was the revolution? Cárdenas broke down and wept.

For More Information

Oster, Patrick. *The Mexicans: A Personal Portrait of a People.* New York: Harper and Row, 1990.

Paz, Octavio. *The Labyrinth of Solitude and Other Writings.* New York: Grove Press, 1985.

Riding, Alan. *Distant Neighbors: A Portrait of the Mexicans.* New York: Vintage Books, 1989.

Ruiz, Ramon Eduardo. *Triumphs and Tragedy: A History of the Mexican People.* New York: W. W. Norton, 1992.

Townsend, William Cameron. *Lázaro Cárdenas: Mexican Democrat.* Ann Arbor, Michigan: George Wahr, 1952.

Experimentation in the Arts

1901
▼
Pablo Picasso begins his "Blue Period."

1902
▼
Igor Stravinsky leaves Russian Conservatory and begins study with Nikolai Rimsky-Korsakov.

1905
▼
Bloody Sunday signals the start of the Russian Revolution, a response to the tyranny of Nicholas II.

1906
▼
Picasso introduces cubism with his painting *Les Demoiselles d'Avignon*.

1910
▼
Stravinsky introduces "primitive music" in the ballet *The Firebird*.

1914
▼
World War I begins.

1918
▼
Stravinsky introduces *The Soldier's Tale*. **Bertolt Brecht** introduces *Baal*.

1926
▼
Brecht produces *Mann ist Mann* and names his dramatic style "epic theater."

1933
▼
Nazis take control of Germany.

1939
▼
World's Fair exhibits Picasso's *Guernica*, which protests the actions of Spanish dictator Francisco Franco.

1947
▼
Brecht answers charges of communism before the U.S. House Un-American Activities Committee.

EXPERIMENTATION IN THE ARTS

The last quarter of the nineteenth century and the first decade of the twentieth marked a period of relative peace. Unrest remained in Russia, where discontent with the ruling Romanov family continued to grow. For the most part, however, this time in history was distinguished by renewed examination of the various systems humanity uses to order the world. Not long before, Charles Darwin had shaken the foundations on which the old order stood by proclaiming the doctrine of evolution (or the ability of species to change over time). Then, as the last quarter of the nineteenth century began, Sigmund Freud rocked the intellectual world again with his inward searching, which led to the establishment of psychoanalysis.

Revolution in art. During this era of inquiry, artists sought to reflect the changes they saw transforming society. They began to challenge long-held concepts of painting and sculpture. Frequently artists sought to make art meaningful in and of itself, rather than for the subjects it represented. Artists felt free to express their own feelings in innovative styles. The painting school of impressionism, which offered an abstract "impression" of a scene rather than a more realistic, near-photographic representation, originated in the 1870s and then gave way to even more abstract forms. The Spaniard **Pablo Picasso** became one

▲ When Pablo Picasso introduced cubism in his 1907 work *Les Demoiselles d'Avignon*, a portrait of five prostitutes, he began a revolution in art.

of the leading experimentalists in art. Eventually, he fled Spain and moved to Paris, then the center of artistic activity. In attempting to represent the three-dimensional world on a flat canvas, he developed a modern style of painting called cubism. In this method, the subject of a work was rendered in geometric shapes made of bold color, often with several views of a subject presented at the same time. When Picasso introduced cubism in his 1907 work *Les Demoiselles d'Avignon,* a portrait of five prostitutes, he began a revolution in art.

Music. Experimentation in music was also widespread during this period. Rebelling against fixed ideas about tone, harmony, and rhythm, musicians such as Claude Debussy adopted the ideas of impressionism to create new styles. In Russia, where the government directed and controlled musical organizations, such experimentation was strongly discouraged. One musician among many who rebelled was **Igor Stravinsky.** His music for ballet rejected traditional models of composition, thus giving the form a new appearance and bringing it increased popularity. His work was so consistent with the prevailing style in the visual arts that for a time he even teamed with Picasso in artistic productions—Stravinsky providing music, Picasso creating stage settings.

Drama. As the new century wore on, tensions that would develop into war grew more pronounced. Dramatists in Germany turned to the new doctrines of Karl Marx for inspiration, hoping to foster progress in society as well as in theater. **Bertolt Brecht** was chief among them. Brecht felt that drama should not only entertain an audience, but provoke it to reflect on ideas as well. He called his method "epic theater." As Germany moved toward war, Marxism was increasingly perceived as a threat to the ruling order. Brecht was forced to flee his native land. He relocated to Hollywood, where his creativity was suppressed by the mainstream, commercial demands of the new motion picture industry. Brecht's earlier experiments with production techniques, however, would have an enormous influence on future playwrights and eventually lead to the Theater of the Absurd, in which human experience is seen as chaotic and without purpose.

Bertolt Brecht

1898-1956

Personal Background

Early life. Eugen Berthold Friedrich Brecht was born in Augsburg, Germany, on February 10, 1898. His parents had moved there from the Black Forest region of southwest Germany soon after their marriage. In Augsburg, Brecht's father, Friedrich Bertold Brecht, took a job in a paper factory and rose to become manager of the plant. He was a Catholic. Brecht's mother, Sophie (Brezing) Brecht, was a Lutheran. In the Brecht family, Sophie's religion won out—young Eugen Berthold was raised a Lutheran, though his faith was never devout.

Brecht grew up in a middle-class home and attended the local school. He later described his early school days at the Augsburg Realgymnasium, remarking, "I did not succeed in imparting any worthwhile education to my teachers. My sense of leisure and independence was tirelessly fostered by them" (Brecht in Hill, p. 22). From his early teens, Brecht preferred writing poetry to doing schoolwork. His only real successes in school were in German composition and Latin. He was growing to be a tall, shy young man, not particularly handsome, but gifted with many friends—and already possessed of a way with women.

Poet. Several years before he left the Augsburg Realgymnasium, Brecht began to establish a reputation as a writer, also indicating an interest in theater. He turned to poetry early, and then,

▲ Bertolt Brecht

Event: Developing "epic theater."

Role: Bertolt Brecht was a German poet and playwright who wrote and produced plays that he hoped would instruct as well as entertain. His goal was to make audiences think about what might be, rather than what was. In 1926 he named his experiments "epic theater." His work, influenced by German social theorist Karl Marx, was often violent and chaotic. It became known throughout the world and would influence generations of playwrights.

at age fifteen, bought a puppet theater with some friends and began to produce plays for parents. Around that time, he helped found a school magazine, *The Harvest,* and began to contribute poems, which also made their way to local newspapers. He wrote about the dark side of society—death, illness, and his view of moral decay in Germany—issues most likely brought into focus by the threat of war.

When war erupted in 1914, Brecht was too young to enlist. He was, however, given a job as an aircraft spotter, along with some of his friends. The boys would climb the medieval towers of the city late at night as the troops boarded trains for the battle lines. Brecht began to record his thoughts about war, which were published in a local newspaper as "Augsburg Letters on the War." In the beginning, his writing was filled with patriotic support for the brave soldiers.

Brecht's war writings. Much of Brecht's early writing about the war, however, was filled with biased and inaccurate information. But as the conflict dragged on, firsthand news of the front changed his perspective. A classmate, Rudolph Ludwig Casper Neher, or Cas as Brecht called him, had enlisted in the Fourth Bavarian Field Artillery. His division would lose over half its men in various battles. On short leaves, Cas and Brecht discussed the atrocities of war. Brecht's patriotic sentiment began to disappear as he heard of Cas's experiences. His writing took on an antiwar fervor. In 1915, for example, Brecht wrote "The Flag Cadet," a poem in which a soldier kills five of the enemy but is mortally wounded in the end—symbolic of the futility of war.

By the time he was eligible for military service, Brecht's enthusiasm for it was wavering. He forged his father's signature on papers that helped him delay being drafted; these documents cited that he was still in school and that there were problems at

---

A View of War

By the end of the first month of Brecht's aircraft watch duty, the initial victims of the war had arrived back in Augsburg, and the budding writer was there to record the event:

> We saw the ruins of young men as they were carried past us on that gray day. One had lost both legs. Another an arm. Another, pale as wax, stared up to heaven. And the great single thing that we Germans want is: To guard our honor. To guard our Freedom, to guard ourselves. And that is worth every sacrifice. (Brecht in Fuegi, p. 17)

home. Brecht's mother was losing a battle with cancer. Brecht found solace in drink, brothels, and the racy literature of German philosopher Friedrich Nietzsche.

Close call. In the spring of 1916, Brecht's Latin class at the gymnasium was asked to write an essay on a line by the Roman poet Horace, "Dulce et decorum est pro patria morio." ("It is sweet and proper to die for your fatherland.") Brecht wrote that it was all well and good for older men to champion going to war, but it was the young men who paid the price. His paper claimed, "Only those whose own heads are completely hollow could carry barefaced trickery so far as to speak of a gentle jump through the doors of darkness" (Brecht in Fuegi, p. 22).

Brecht's strong language outraged his Latin instructor, who demanded that he be expelled from school. But Brecht's French teacher, Father Sauer, stepped in and pleaded for him. Father Sauer saved Brecht from expulsion and an earlier draft, possibly saving his life.

In 1917 Brecht finished his secondary schooling and enrolled at the University of Munich, supposedly to study medicine. But he had no interest in the subject and did not plan to become a doctor; he simply enrolled because his father wanted him to and because he still needed to avoid the draft. Brecht's real plan was to sign up for several courses in the medical program, let his father pay the tuition, then drop the classes and keep the money for himself. He chose to remain in classes about the Bible and theater.

Participation: Developing "Epic Theater"

Baal. On a challenge and a boast, Brecht announced that he could write a play in three days. The announcement came as a jealous reaction to the success of a play by another playwright, Hanns Johst.

Baal, Brecht's first full-length drama, took much more than three days to write. In fact, it took several months even with the help of friends. The play seemed to include elements of Brecht's own life—seduction, bisexuality, and daring—along with direct quotes from famous writers such as fifteenth-century French poet François Villon and nineteenth-century American poet Walt Whitman, among others—all used without acknowledging their sources. Nonetheless, with *Baal,* Brecht began trying to make money from the theater, while also using it to teach and encourage debate.

The end of the war. In the fall of 1918, Brecht was finally forced to join the German army. Even then, he was shielded from actual combat, as his assignment took him into the medical corps. In four months, Brecht saw no fighting action, nor many, if any, war casualties. He was assigned to a clinic near his home that treated patients with venereal diseases. The end of the war terminated his service. Brecht had successfully avoided the fate of thirty million people who had been captured, wounded, or lost in action, as well as the approximately nine million who lost their lives in World War I, then called "The Great War."

A Critic on *Baal*

"It is both a literary and a social protest...; Baal (like Brecht) plays the guitar, writes poetry, eats, drinks, dances, makes love, and uses and drops people without scruples.... As an affront against a stale society, Baal breaks conventions at every turn, living only for his own pleasure, indulging until the last moment in the sensual experiences of this world which knows no afterworld" (Mews, p. 124).

The end of the war brought chaos to Germany. Revolutionaries had united to form the Communist Party of Germany, which sought to overthrow the ruling class. The most radical faction of the party called for outright battle and named itself Spartacides, after Spartacus, a famous rebel slave in ancient Rome. Eventually, the army succeeded in putting down the communist movement, but only by resorting to brutality.

Brecht and his friend Cas followed the rebellion and began working on a play about the failure of the Spartacides. The result, *Drums in the Night,* is comprised mostly of songs that Brecht had been singing in taverns. In one, "The Legend of the Dead Soldier," a deceased soldier is resurrected to serve once again for his country. The main character, Baal, decides to abandon the revolution and act on his own impulses. Brecht's hatred of war and his belief that society was in need of reform is forcefully presented. The play brought Brecht recognition and controversy. It also won the national Kleist Award in 1922. In 1924 Brecht was offered a job as playwright for the Deutsches Theater under the world-renowned director Max Rinehardt. He moved to Berlin and for nearly a decade wrote plays about his unhappiness with society.

"Epic Theater." By 1926 Brecht was achieving widespread acclaim. He strengthened his commitment to producing plays that educated first and earned money second. To this end, he boldly used language that had not been part of the theater before. In fact, almost every aspect of his productions were positioned to provoke thought in audiences. His complex works often sent theatergoers a disguised message. Sometimes one actor played several different roles. Sometimes silence prevailed onstage. The aim was to take observers out of the realm of reality and place them in a position in which they would be forced to contemplate a better society; his theories stressed the arousal of a critical response by alienating the spectator from the staged action. Brecht had been working toward this technique all his writing life. He gave it the name "epic theater."

Brecht's epic theater was often violent, chaotic, and confusing. In the plays that reached this level, he was prefiguring the Theater of the Absurd, in which human experience is seen as without purpose.

Marxism. In 1926, while researching economics for some new plays he was planning, Brecht read German political philosopher Karl Marx's *Das Kapital*. Soon after, he claimed to have adopted communism. (In fact, acquaintances found little evidence that he actually understood the economics of *Das Kapital*.) Brecht began to associate with Communist Party members in Germany. Like his newfound comrades, he was growing increasingly alarmed at the advances of a young National Socialist, or Nazi, leader, Adolf Hitler. Brecht's poems took on an even darker tone—often condoning whatever was required, including murder and incitement to riot, to achieve a higher good.

Brecht and Women

Brecht had an easy way with women, whom he freely wooed and as freely used. He had two sons by two different women with whom he collaborated in playwriting. His second marriage was to an actress who tolerated his open relationships with other women. One affair was with Elisabeth Hauptmann, who loved Brecht and hoped to marry him. She helped him write his third successful play, *A Man's a Man*, but received no credit for her work. Later, when Brecht moved to the United States, he brought his wife and two mistresses with him.

▲ Brecht and his wife Helene Weigel in Copenhagen, Denmark, during the fall of 1936.

In 1929 Brecht finished one of this greatest works, *The Threepenny Opera*. Once again the playwright sought to question middle-class society. *The Threepenny Opera* brought Brecht even more fame and wealth. It had become Brecht's habit to work with a composer in the development of his work. He created this play with composer Kurt Weill. And though the musical would later be recognized as something of a masterwork for the writer, international acclaim for *The Threepenny Opera* was generally more for Weill's catchy tunes than for Brecht's characters.

Aftermath

Hitler. In 1933 Hitler led the Nazis to power. Brecht had been on the Nazi blacklist for some time for dishonoring German soldiers. When Hitler ordered the burning of government buildings, Brecht feared for his life and fled to Prague, Czechoslovakia. His journey in exile took him to Switzerland, Denmark, Sweden, and Russia. He eventually traveled by ship to the United States.

The United States. For eight years—from the outbreak of World War II in 1939 until 1947—Brecht lived in the United States. In that time, he worked on several motion picture productions and wrote three plays. But his work in America was not warmly received, and Brecht did not receive the United States warmly, either. He never applied for citizenship. It was perhaps inevitable that he would be called before the communist-hunting House Un-American Activities Committee and questioned about his communist connections. Almost immediately, he left the United States to return to Germany. When asked by a friend if he had indeed done anything "un-American," Brecht is said to have replied, "I am not an American." He chose to live in communist East Berlin. He and his wife Helene Weigel founded a theater company there, the Berliner Ensemble, where Brecht produced his own plays as well as adaptations of the works of William Shakespeare and Molière.

> ### Brecht's Will
>
> Though Brecht left control of his estate to his wife Helene Weigel, as well as bequests for his daughter, Barbara, and son, Stefan, his will awarded some of his wealth to several women. Kathie Reichel was given a house, provided she act in one of his plays; Mrs. Isot Kilian received royalties from his songs; Ruth Berlau, a one-time lover, received fifty thousand Danish kroner to buy a house that would go to Helene when Ruth died.

Gradually, however, Brecht's health began to fail. He died on August 14, 1956. His will left control of his estate to his wife, but it also provided for several other women—always with provisions that they perform some duty in return.

For More Information

Fuegi, John. *Brecht and Co.* New York: Grove, 1994.

Hill, Claude. *Bertolt Brecht.* Boston: Twayne, 1975.

Willett, John. *Bertolt Brecht Short Stories, 1921-1946.* New York: Chaucer, 1983.

Pablo Picasso

1881-1973

Personal Background

Early Years. Pablo Ruiz y Picasso was born on October 25, 1881, in Malaga, Spain, to José Ruiz and his wife, Maria Picasso. Two weeks later he was baptized Pablo Diego José Francisco de Paula Juan Nepomuceno Maria de los Remedios Cipriano de la Santisima Trinidad Picasso Ruiz.

Picasso learned early on how to draw and paint. His teacher was his father, an art instructor at the School of Arts and Crafts of San Telmo and also the curator of the city museum. José Ruiz's painting was limited to still lifes and pigeons, but he was able to pass on a passion for art to his son. That passion would become the driving force of Picasso's life.

Beginning artist. In 1891 José Ruiz moved his family to Corunna, a seaport on the Atlantic Coast, where he had accepted a teaching position at the La Guardia Institute. It was at Corunna that Picasso began experimenting with a technique called chiaroscuro—using light and dark areas to create shadow—in charcoal paintings. Within a year his painting had developed to the point where he was able to produce his own magazines, providing both art and text. His desire to paint and draw was so great that he would sometimes finish paintings for his father. José soon recognized his son's enormous talent.

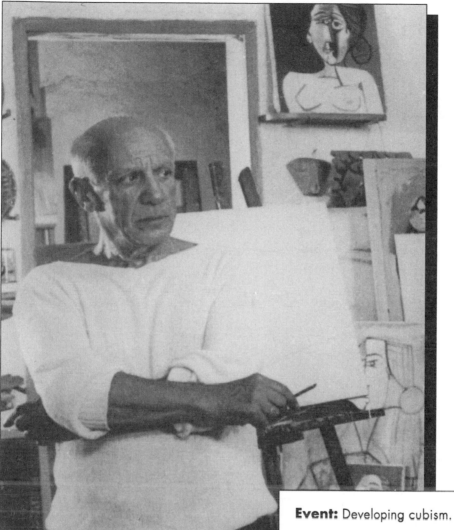

▲ **Pablo Picasso**

Event: Developing cubism.

Role: Pablo Picasso was a Spanish-born painter, sculptor, and printmaker who is widely considered the greatest artist of the twentieth century. He sparked a revolution in art with his use of geometric figures to represent his subjects, a style called cubism.

Art education. In 1895 an opening became available at the La Lonja School of Fine Arts in Barcelona, and José Ruiz accepted the position. José then asked school officials to give Picasso a chance to test for admission. The test consisted of two charcoal drawings of living models. They would be judged for realism and precision. Most candidates took an entire month to complete the two drawings—Picasso finished the examination in just one week and, at the age of fifteen, was quickly admitted.

Pronounced Stillborn

Incredibly, Picasso was abandoned by the midwife who attended his mother. The midwife believed the infant was stillborn, but the baby's uncle, Salvador, who was a doctor, blew smoke in the baby's nose, causing him to cough and breathe, thereby saving him.

Picasso had the complete support of his family when he later applied to the Royal Academy of San Fernando in Madrid—perhaps the most important art school of the time. Picasso was accepted to the school, but he had learned that the course of study there was very rigid and formal. Then, too, his own familiar Barcelona had many attractions for a young painter. Barcelona was a thriving center of trade through which new ideas flowed from all over Europe, particularly from Germany. German writers and philosophers were developing new approaches to the arts and sciences. The young painter also believed he would have more personal freedom in Barcelona than in Madrid. Picasso, therefore, refused the offer to attend the Royal Academy. Instead, he and a friend shared a studio on the Calle Riera de San Juan, a street in Barcelona.

Surpassed Father

One evening when Picasso's father, José Ruiz, was feeling melancholy, he turned the painting he was working on over to his son and went for a walk. When he returned, the pigeons in the painting were finished and were so astonishingly true to life that Don José was moved to give young Pablo his pallet and brushes. He then announced that his son's talent had superseded his own and that from then on, he would paint no more.

Paris. Even with its highly charged atmosphere, Barcelona did not hold the two young artists long. In 1900, at the age of nineteen, Picasso and his friend moved to Paris. There they adopted the look popular with hungry young artists—shabby clothes and long hair. When they returned to Malaga, Spain, for the Christmas holidays, they were greeted with disdain because of their new appearances. The rejection, however, seemed only to build confidence and self-assurance in Picasso. He

▲ *Gertrude Stein;* Picasso painted this portrait of his friend and patron Gertrude Stein in 1906, during his Blue Period.

soon moved to Madrid, where an exciting new period of his work began.

Blue Period. In the fall of 1901, Picasso began to produce paintings that strongly revealed his own feelings. His artist friend had moved back to Paris and shortly thereafter committed suicide over a failed love. Picasso fell into a period of self-examination and melancholy. During this period of his life, now known as the "Blue Period," he began to turn away from impressions of the gay cafe life and outdoor scenes. Picasso portrayed the depths of city life—prostitutes, beggars, cripples, the homeless and outcast. The bright hues of his earlier works were replaced with pale and somber colors. Strong lines seemed to emphasize the coldness of the scenes.

Picasso's dominant color was blue. For example, one of his paintings depicts an old man weakly holding a guitar. Set against a bare background, Picasso emphasizes the dejected, isolated spirit of the man. This picture, *The Old Guitarist,* ably illustrates Picasso's growing sensitivity in the Blue Period. The work was painted just before he threw off his depression and moved once more. It was during the Blue Period that he began to sign his work "Picasso," taking his mother's surname, which was not uncommon in Spain.

Rose Period. In 1903 Picasso left Spain for good. He and a fellow artist made the journey to Paris. Along the way Picasso painted a series of sketches something like a comic strip; he showed his renewed enthusiasm for life by naming them "Alleluia."

Picasso moved into an apartment at 13 rue Ravignon. It was in a broken-down building in a section of Paris called Montmartre. Laundry barges had long docked nearby on the Seine, and another resident, writer Max Jacob, had named the place Bateau Lavoir (Laundry Boat) after the barges. The building, nearly uninhabitable and lacking plumbing, would be Picasso's home for five years. Heat in the summer was unbearable as was cold in winter.

Picasso was as poor as those he had painted during his Blue Period, but he found a richness of life in his friends and his own revived spirit. He became close to many people who would eventually have a direct impact on his work. Max Jacob was one of these friends. The son of a Jewish tailor and antique dealer, he had grown up in ridicule because of his faith. Jacob and Picasso began to meet daily, communicating—because they spoke different languages—through pantomime. They developed a deep and genuine friendship. Among his other acquaintances was Gertrude Stein, an American writer, and her brother, Theo. The already successful Stein bought more than thirty Picasso paintings.

Also during these years, Picasso fell in love with a neighbor, Fernande Olivier, who became the first of many mistresses and subjects of his paintings. Olivier did not find him particularly handsome but was drawn to his striking black eyes, which seemed to radiate the passion within the artist. She soon moved in with him and was charged with the responsibility of cooking. She was not allowed to leave the apartment unless accompanied by the very possessive Picasso.

Earthy browns, tender rose hues, and warm, human tones filled Picasso's paintings from 1904 to 1906. He was fascinated by the loneliness and gentleness of circus people. He painted the performers dressed in their bright costumes and accompanied by their animals. The solitary figures of the earlier paintings gave way to the celebration of life in a period called the "Rose Period." His figures were no longer placed in an empty and lifeless setting, but with pets, friends, and family members, giving the works a sense of compassion and optimism. The artist also began to experiment with sculpture. His first piece, *Harlequin*, was completed in 1905. He would soon create an entirely new style of painting.

Picasso's Pets

While Picasso was living in a building called Bateau Lavoir (Laundry Boat) in the Montmartre section of Paris, he had two pets—a white mouse and a big yellow dog named Frika.

Participation: Developing Cubism

Success. By 1906 Picasso had become a successful, recognized artist. His paintings were in great demand among art collectors, and his circle held him in the highest professional esteem.

The acclaim gave Picasso greater confidence in his creative skills. That year he began work on a painting that would mark a turning point not only in Picasso's own growth as an artist but as a revolutionary in the art world. This single painting is said to have changed the course of art. It was titled *Les Demoiselles d'Avignon*.

Earlier Picasso paintings had been in the style of impressionism, which had prevailed since the 1870s. Using primary colors and short brush stokes, the impressionists concentrated on a general "impression" of a scene rather than photographically rendered details. The new picture, named for a brothel on Barcelona's Avignon Street, portrayed five nude women gathered around an arrangement of fruit. The painting employed a new style developed by Picasso and his friend Georges Braque. In *Les Demoiselles,* the idea of realistic representation was abandoned. Instead, the figures are depicted in flat, geometric shapes.

Picasso had prepared thoroughly for this painting. He had made more than thirty-one preliminary sketches in various mediums including charcoal, pencil, watercolor, and oil. The result was something completely new in Western art. Picasso was twenty-five years old when he unveiled *Les Demoiselles d'Avignon,* which created an uproar in the art community. Exhibited by Picasso's dealer, it was reviewed by the well-known art critic Louis Vauxcelles. He commented that the pictures were made up of nothing but cubes. The style, therefore, became known as "cubism." Besides the geometric shapes, paintings in this style were characterized by harsh, bold lines. Part of the philosophy behind this method was to divorce pieces of art from reality; each painting in the new style would have a reality of its own. The artists did not even add their signatures to their work.

Success of cubism. Cubism was shocking to the art community. Braque and Picasso recognized this and did not take their work lightly. Each evening they would visit one another to see what had been produced that day. A piece of art was not complete until both artists agreed that it was. Objects were painted not as they appeared, but as they were broken down structurally. It was an exploration of space, volume, and order. Sometimes the subjects appeared as if viewed from all angles at the same time.

▲ *Guernica,* which Picasso painted in 1937 to protest the bombing of the undefended Basque town during the Spanish Civil War.

By 1912 Picasso had begun expanding cubism into other art mediums—creating works of newspaper, sand, and wallpaper, for example. The invention of collage and papier collé (a technique of pasting scraps of paper onto a canvas) moved cubism in new directions. But world events were soon to turn the artist to other ventures.

Aftermath

World War I. In 1914 a war began in Europe that would engulf much of the world. Most of Picasso's friends enlisted to fight or left Paris. One again the great artist was alone. The dominance of cubism began to fade. Different subjects required different styles of expression, he believed, and cubism now took its place as just one of many means of airing the artist's ideas and emotions. In 1917 he was asked to design sets for the Russian Ballet. He followed that experience by creating sets for other directors and composers, including **Igor Stravinsky** (see entry).

Spanish Civil War. In the 1930s, Picasso's works became more symbolic of the tragedy of the times. He was outraged by the inhumanity of the Spanish Civil War and expressed his anger in a series of etchings called *The Dream and the Lie of Franco* and in *Guernica,* a huge mural portraying the bombing of a small town by dictator Francisco Franco's forces. Picasso chose to show this disaster on a massive scale, in a painting eleven feet by twenty-five feet in size. Its imagery includes a dying horse, a mother holding her dead baby, and screaming animals and people.

World War II. On September 1, 1939, German armies invaded Poland, and France joined England in a declaration of war on the aggressors. Rumors spread that Paris would be bombed by the Germans, and Picasso fled to Royan. There he continued to paint through the early part of the war, using his bathroom as a studio since it was the only heated room in the residence. A year later, when German troops began to occupy France, the artist was invited to move to the United States or Mexico.

Guernica

At 4:40 in the afternoon of April 26, 1937, German planes flying in the service of Francisco Franco bombed the undefended Basque town of Guernica. Franco struck at the busiest time of a market day, when people crowded the streets. The town held no strategic value for Franco, and the act vividly demonstrated the disregard for human values in the war. The Spanish republican government, an elected body overthrown by Franco in 1936, commissioned Picasso to paint a large canvas of this disaster to be displayed at the 1939 World's Fair.

But Picasso decided to return to Paris as a statement of protest against the war. The move did not go unnoticed by the Germans; German Nazi leader Adolf Hitler announce that Picasso was a bad influence. His work was banned and German soldiers frequently searched his studio—several, however, took time to ask for his autograph. He was able to continue his work only with the help of friends, who smuggled materials to him at night. A grand exhibit of his work after the war displayed seventy-four paintings and five sculptures.

Picasso went on to become the most successful artist of the twentieth century. In 1967 he sold *Mother and Child at the Seashore,* a painting made during his Blue Period, for $532,000. At the time, it was the highest price ever paid for a single work by a living artist.

Picasso died in Mougins, France, on April 8, 1973, and was mourned as the last of the great masters.

Gilot, Francoise, and Carlton Lake. *Life with Picasso*. Garden City, New York: Doubleday, 1989.

Jaffe, Hans. *Picasso*. New York: Abrams, 1983.

Porzio, Domenico. *Understanding Picasso*. New York: Newsweek Books, 1974.

Rewald, J. *Post-Impressionism*. 3rd edition. New York: Abrams, 1962.

Rewald, J. *The History of Impressionism*. Revised 4th edition. New York: Abrams, 1990.

Wertenbaker, Lael. *The World of Picasso, 1881—*. New York: Time-Life Books, 1967.

Igor Stravinsky

1882-1971

Personal Background

Igor Fyodorovich Stravinsky was born on June 17, 1882, in Oranienbaum, Russia, a summer resort on the Gulf of Finland and a short railway ride from St. Petersburg. Stravinsky was born into a musical environment; his father, Fyodor, sang lead bass in operas at the Mariinsky Theatre in St. Petersburg. When the boy was eleven, he saw the performance of Glinka's *Ruslan and Lyudmila,* with his father on stage as Farlaf. Stravinsky later recorded in his diaries that on this occasion something special happened:

> It was my good fortune to catch a glimpse in the foyer of Peter Tchaikovsky, the idol of the Russian public.... He had just conducted the first audition of his new symphony, the *Pathetic,* in St. Petersburg. A fortnight later my mother took me to a concert where the same symphony was played in memory of the composer, who had been suddenly carried off by cholera.... I was far from realizing at the moment [that] that glimpse of the living Tchaikovsky—fleeting though it was—would become one of my most treasured memories. (Stravinsky in Peyser, p. 87)

Though Stravinsky was raised in a musical household, his parents stressed the importance of education and felt that music should be secondary. But Stravinsky gained support for his pursuit of music from his uncle Alexander Yelachich, whom he later remembered as a forward-thinking man with strong opinions about art and politics. At age nine Stravinsky began studying the

▲ Igor Stravinsky

Event: Creating a new music.

Role: Russian-born American composer Igor Stravinsky is widely considered one of the great geniuses of modern music. His innovations in tone, rhythm, and harmony were revolutionary in their day, and his compositions have been universally acclaimed.

piano with a pupil of the brilliant pianist Anton Rubenstein. Rubenstein was the director of the Moscow Conservatory of Music, which, by governmental requirement, was oriented toward very formal Russian music. His student—Stravinsky's teacher—refused to allow Stravinsky to improvise; he was forced to learn to play the standard European works of such artists as Felix Mendelssohn, Wolfgang Amadeus Mozart, Ludwig van Beethoven, Joseph Haydn, and others.

Despite these limitations, Stravinsky spent a great deal of time practicing and became technically proficient at the piano. His studies continued under the German Vassily Kalafaty, who taught his young student to rely on his ear—to be less mechanical—in making musical judgments. It was a lesson Stravinsky was happy to learn. At fifteen, Stravinsky met Ivan Pokrovsky and was introduced to French music. Thus Stravinsky received an international education in music and was influenced by a variety of instructors. Still, he felt that the emphasis on formal styles in his training had caused his own musical creativity to ripen in ignorance.

The Moscow Conservatory. Many Russian students came to study at the Moscow Conservatory of Music under the direction of Rubenstein. The professors at the conservatory, heeding a directive from the Russian government, discouraged pupils from taking an interest in the influence of foreign music. As a result Stravinsky found the conservatory too rigid and looked elsewhere for inspiration. He began attending "Evenings of Contemporary Music," an organization that played French music. Meanwhile, to please his parents, he became a law student at the University of St. Petersburg.

Rimsky-Korsakov. In 1902 Stravinsky was vacationing with his family in Heidelberg, Germany, when he approached composer Nikolai Rimsky-Korsakov and asked for composition lessons. He was advised to study harmony and counterpoint further and to steer clear of the conservatory. Stravinsky began studying with Rimsky-Korsakov twice a week. A few months later, Stravinsky's father died of cancer, and Rimsky-Korsakov assumed a more paternal role. By 1903 Stravinsky had become a regular member of Rimsky-Korsakov's circle. He was still studying law when he began to compose his first symphony, *Opus I*.

While Stravinsky was developing his musical talent, the czarist empire reached the brink of disaster. In 1904 Russia went to war with Japan and was defeated at sea. Compounding this defeat, the government was too weak to resist Austrian claims to some Russian territory. Discontent grew among the workers. By October 1905, demonstrations and strikes were being organized against the government. By the end of that year, the czar gave in to the demands of the people for a parliamentary voice. Czar Nicholas II, however, had no intention of allowing the new parliament any real say in the government. Still, for a brief time, technology and humanism prospered. Writers such as Leo Tolstoy, Ivan Bunin, and others explored new directions in literature, and Russian ballet, under the direction of Sergei Diaghilev, became one of the most profound artistic forces of the century.

Marriage and a career in music. In 1906 Stravinsky graduated from law school. He was twenty-three and certain that he wanted to become a composer. A year later he married his cousin, Catherine Nossenko, and moved to Ustilug in the province of Volhynia in southern Russia. There Stravinsky worked on a musical piece to celebrate the approaching marriage of Rimsky-Korsakov's daughter. But much to Stravinsky's distress, Rimsky-Korsakov died shortly thereafter, without ever having heard the piece.

The Russia of Stravinsky's Youth

Igor Stravinsky grew up in an atmosphere of social turmoil. In 1884 the government of Russia had attempted land reform. It appointed "land captains" who took charge of all peasant affairs. The change led to widespread confusion. Also that year, the government reinforced its practice of banning children of working-class parents from attending grammar school. This repression inspired calls for freedom from the domination of the czar. The arts, however, flourished even as Russia began a period of great unrest. Although censorship by government authorities prevailed, operas, plays, and concerts were plentiful. St. Petersburg, one of the most beautiful cities in the world, attracted notable musicians and artists from all over the world.

Three years later, two of Stravinsky's works, *Scherzo fantastique* and *Feu d'artifice,* were performed at a concert directed by the leading Russian conductor at that time, Alexander Siloti. Sergei Diaghilev, director of the Moscow ballet, was present in the audience and was so impressed by the music that he asked Stravinsky to score pieces by Fréderic Chopin for a ballet performance of *Les Sylphides.*

Participation: Creating a New Music

The Firebird. Stravinsky's involvement with Diaghilev led to several opportunities. Toward the end of 1909, the ballet master Mikhail Fokine was developing a ballet based on familiar Russian folktales for Diaghilev's Ballet Russe. The ballet centered around the image of the firebird, a phoenix. The phoenix is a mythical bird that rises from its ashes after death and is often used as a symbol of rebirth in works of art and literature. Stravinsky was offered the chance to compose when Anatol Liadov, then a more prominent composer, failed to deliver a score on time.

Stravinsky wrote the music to *The Firebird* in a form called *ballet d'action,* in which the music follows the action on the stage bar for bar. The Ballet Russe was on the cutting edge of the arts, incorporating music, dance, and scenic stage design as equal parts of the production. Painter **Pablo Picasso** (see entry) designed sets for *The Firebird* in his revolutionary cubist style. The combination of Picasso's sets and Stravinsky's score created a stir in the art world.

The debut of *The Firebird* took place on June 25, 1910, at the Paris Opera House and was dedicated to Rimsky-Korsakov. The conductor was Frenchmen Gabriel Pierne, and the production team was entirely Russian. Reaction to *The Firebird* was positive, and it became popular almost immediately. This propelled Stravinsky into the spotlight and brought him in direct contact with composers Maurice Ravel, Claude Debussy, and others. In June 1915, Stravinsky made his debut as a conductor, leading an orchestra in *The Firebird* in Paris.

Petrushka. While finishing *The Firebird* in St. Petersburg, Stravinsky had experienced a vision: an image of a young girl, surrounded by elders, who dances herself to death. In composing music to fit this image, he conceived of a puppet, suddenly given

▶

Stravinsky and dancer and choreographer Vaslav Nijinsky, costumed as Petrushka for Stravinsky's ballet, circa 1911; in order to present the human and mechanical elements of Petrushka's personality, Stravinsky created a bitonal chord that has since become famous.

life. Diaghilev was intrigued by the imagery and decided to include it in a ballet.

In the summer of 1910, Stravinsky moved his family to Lausanne, Switzerland, where he began work on *Petrushka*. The story involves a magician and three puppets. The plot entails the refusal of Petrushka (one of the puppets) to be controlled by the magician's strings. In order to present the human and mechanical elements of Petrushka's personality, Stravinsky created a bitonal chord (a simultaneous use of two different keys) that has since become famous. This chord would be heard for the first time in *Petrushka*.

The ballet is set in Admiralty Square in St. Petersburg during the celebration of carnival in about 1830. Many interpreted *Petrushka* as a moral statement on the times, claiming that the unstable political and social climate was depicted onstage, but with a magical twist.

Petrushka was completed on May 26, 1911, and opened on June 13, at the Théâtre du Chatelet in Paris. *Petrushka* and *The Firebird* established Stravinsky's reputation in every major city; the art world awaited his next move with excitement.

The Rite of Spring. Stravinsky's third ballet, *The Rite of Spring,* was performed on May 29, 1913, at the Théâtre des Champs-Elysées in Paris and marked a complete departure from contemporary music. The work was choreographed and danced by the great Vaslav Nijinsky. The orchestra was the largest Stravinsky had ever conducted. It consisted primarily of wind instruments and drums. The ballet, directed by Pierre Monteux, is considered the most astounding first performance of any musical work of the early twentieth century.

But the work that brought Stravinsky such acclaim also inspired controversy. Reaction to *The Rite of Spring* resulted in a public protest, and fights broke out between supporters and opponents of Stravinsky. Opponents criticized it for shunning traditional values in music. Indeed, Stravinsky's concepts of composition and his unorthodox approach to tone, harmony, and rhythm were astounding at the time. He is viewed by many as one of the earliest modern composers.

Brink of war. Stravinsky sought refuge in Switzerland a few weeks before the onset of World War I. The war brought an end to the cultural supremacy of Paris, where Stravinsky had made his reputation. During the war, Stravinsky was in close contact with Diaghilev, who coordinated events for the Red Cross in Geneva, Switzerland, and Paris. He also associated with many great artists, including Picasso and the French writer, artist, and filmmaker Jean Cocteau. Picasso painted Stravinsky in 1920.

Throughout the war, Stravinsky worked on musical scores that were derived from Russian folklore. He produced the short opera *Renard,* the dance cantata *Les Noces,* and *The Soldier's Tale,* which was first introduced in Lausanne in 1918. The performance involved a reader, an instrumental ensemble, and dancers. The production was a hit, and Stravinsky planned to take it to other cities, but this plan was canceled due to an epidemic of influenza that swept across Europe. Nevertheless, Stravinsky's fame continued to spread throughout the world.

Aftermath

Russian Revolution. The Russian Revolution of 1917 brought an end to czarist rule. The Bolsheviks (Communist Party extremists) seized control of the nation, and communism became the governing force. In 1939 Stravinsky left Europe and settled in the United States. By 1945, when he became an American citizen, he was firmly positioned in the musical establishment of his new home. Stravinsky would return to Russia only once, in 1962.

Death. Igor Stravinsky died on April 6, 1971, in New York City. He was buried in the Russian corner of San Michele cemetery in Venice, Italy, near Sergei Diaghilev.

For More Information

Griffiths, Paul. *The Master Musicians, Stravinsky.* New York: Schirmer, 1992.

Peyser, Joan. *The New Music.* London: Katomo, 1971.

Stravinsky, Igor, and Robert Craft. *Retrospectives and Conclusions.* New York: Alfred A. Knopf, 1969.

World Wars

1914
Austrian archduke Francis Ferdinand is assassinated. Austria-Hungary, encouraged by **Wilhelm II,** declares war on Serbia; Germany declares war on France; Britain on Germany; Russia, France, and Britain on the Ottoman Empire.

1917
The U.S. declares war on Germany; Congresswoman **Jeannette Rankin** votes against entry into the European war. Russia withdraws and is immediately engulfed by communist revolution.

1933
Adolf Hitler takes control of Germany.

1922
Benito Mussolini establishes fascist government in Italy.

1919
Treaty of Versailles sets conditions for peace.

1918
Germany and the Allies agree to an armistice.

1935
Mussolini directs Italian invasion of Ethiopia.

1936
Mussolini and Hitler join to intervene in the Spanish Civil War—beginning of the Axis.

1939
World War II begins as Germany invades Poland. France and Britain declare war on Germany. Soviet Union invades Poland.

1940
Charles de Gaulle flees France; establishes Free French government in exile in England.

1945
Germany surrenders; U.S. drops atom bombs on Japan; Japan surrenders. Wallenberg disappears in Soviet custody.

1944
Allies invade German-occupied France. Sweden and U.S. send **Raoul Wallenberg** to rescue Hungarian Jews.

1941
Germany invades Soviet Union; Japanese attack Pearl Harbor. Rankin votes against U.S. declaration of war.

WORLD WARS

The last quarter of the nineteenth century brought great change and unease to Europe. Germany, benefitting from an educational system that produced highly skilled mechanics, had prospered greatly from the Industrial Revolution and began to threaten the balance of power that had existed since 1815. Nations were aligned with one another and realigned according to changing views about how to protect Europe from German domination. Meanwhile, Germany had reason to fear its neighbors as well. War was generally avoided by the major powers throughout this quarter century in large part due to the skillful diplomacy of one of the world's greatest leaders, German chancellor Otto von Bismarck.

A series of alliances, many of them engineered by Bismarck, held the threat of large-scale war at bay until the twentieth century. In 1890 Bismarck was dismissed by a new German kaiser, **Wilhelm II,** and the stability that had been provided by Germany began to deteriorate. The irresponsible and short-sighted policies of Wilhelm II led directly to the outbreak of World War I. The kaiser withdrew Germany from its reinsurance (nonaggression) pact with Russia, encouraging Russia to form an alliance with France, Germany's enemy. His foolhardy expansion of the German navy antagonized England. Wilhelm

II also challenged France's interest in Morocco, losing the challenge and gaining no friends for Germany. A tense Europe soon erupted into a series of skirmishes in which Bulgaria and Romania challenged the Ottoman Empire. The Balkan wars, as they were called, further divided the European nations. Russia and Austria-Hungary, both close to the wars, were upset with Britain and Germany for not becoming involved. Germany and Britain, meanwhile, struggled to keep the support of their allies during this period of nonintervention. Russia sought support in an alliance with France. Just over a decade into the new century, Europeans were sitting on a powder keg ready to explode.

European Alliances	
1879	Defensive alliance between Germany and Austria.
1881	Renewal of the Three Emperors' League—Austria, Germany, and Russia.
1882	Triple Alliance—Germany, Austria, and Italy.
1887	Reinsurance Treaty—Germany and Russia.
1894	Military alliance—France and Germany.
1904	Entente Cordiale—France and Britain.
1907	Triple Entente—France, Britain, and Russia.

June 28, 1914, has been called by some the first day of the twentieth century. On that day, a Bosnian Serb assassinated Archduke Francis Ferdinand, heir to the throne of Austria-Hungary, and his wife in Sarajevo, Bosnia. The event triggered the outbreak of World War I.

Wilhelm II miscalculated when he encouraged Austria-Hungary to launch a punitive (punishing) war against Serbia following the assassination; he believed the war would be confined to Serbia and result in increased influence in the Balkans for Austria-Hungary and its ally, Germany. Instead, Austria-Hungary's attack on Serbia started a world war that ultimately cost the kaiser his throne.

The Treaty of Versailles, which the victorious Allies (primarily Russia, Great Britain, and the United States) imposed on Germany, did not adequately provide for a lasting peace. Instead it created conditions that would lead to another world war in roughly twenty years. The treaty's requirements that Germany cede territory, make huge financial reparations to the Allies, limit its armed forces, and assume sole responsibility for starting the war led to widespread discontent in Germany. This eventually

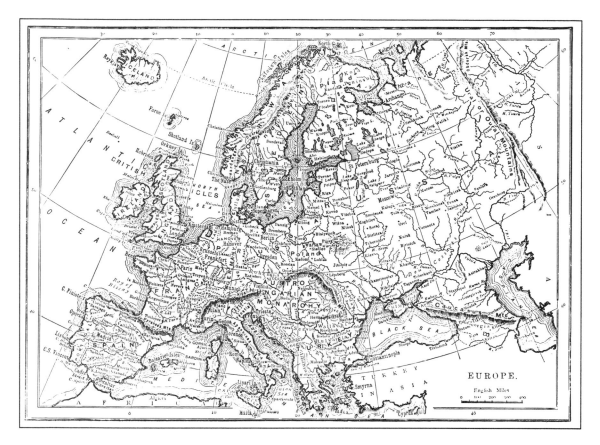

▲ **Europe at the turn of the twentieth century; just over a decade into the new century, Europeans were sitting on a powder keg ready to explode.**

contributed to the rise of Adolf Hitler, who pursued a course of rearmament and territorial expansion after he came to power in 1933.

The Western powers' policy of appeasing Hitler by allowing him to rearm and seize territory in Central and Eastern Europe failed to satisfy him. In 1939, after making a deal with Soviet leader Joseph Stalin, he launched an invasion of Poland. Britain and France declared war on Germany and its partners in aggression. But France was easily overrun by the better-prepared German army. Some French leaders joined the Nazis, while others fled to exile in Britain or North Africa.

▲ **British prime minister Winston Churchill inspects bomb damage in the Battersea area of London the morning after a German raid, 1940; the world wars resulted in tens of millions of deaths and the decline of Europe's great powers.**

Charles de Gaulle, a World War I veteran, led a French armored unit against the Germans when they invaded France in 1940. Later, while serving in the government, he tried to persuade French leaders not to surrender to the Germans. When

France finally did surrender, de Gaulle fled to London. With the help of British prime minister Winston Churchill, he formed a government-in-exile and eventually raised an army of Frenchmen—the Free French—to fight the Germans alongside the British and Americans. But de Gaulle was a prickly character; Churchill and U.S. president Franklin D. Roosevelt would find him a troublesome ally.

The world wars provided numerous examples of individual courage and self-sacrifice. **Jeannette Rankin,** the first woman to be elected to the U.S. Congress, defied pressure from her supporters as well as her detractors when she voted against declaring war on Germany in 1917. In 1941 she was the only officer of Congress to vote against a declaration of war on Japan following the Japanese attack on Pearl Harbor.

Swedish businessman **Raoul Wallenberg** employed his considerable wits and enormous courage to save thousands of Jews from death in Nazi-occupied Hungary during the closing days of the European Theater of World War II. After risking his life on numerous occasions, he was arrested by the Soviets—who believed he was a spy—immediately after they expelled the Nazis from Hungary. Though the truth about his fate was not known, for fifty years, he was killed by the Soviet secret service after refusing repeatedly to become a Soviet spy.

The world wars resulted in tens of millions of deaths, the decline of Europe's great powers, and the emergence of the United States and the Soviet Union as the world's superpowers.

Wilhelm II

1859-1941

Personal Background

Royal and military destiny. Wilhelm II was the son of Princess Victoria and the grandson of Queen Victoria of England. (In 1901 he would hold his grandmother in his arms as she died.) He was born in Berlin, Germany, on January 27, 1859. His father was Crown Prince Friedrich of Prussia. Wilhelm II was therefore born into all the privileges of the Prussian ruling family, the Hohenzollerns.

The birth of Wilhelm II was difficult; it left the infant with his left arm permanently paralyzed and ear injuries that resulted in partial deafness and some loss of balance. These handicaps could well have kept the child from normal activities and certainly would have prevented most other boys from entering the military service expected of a future emperor. Wilhelm, however, learned to cope with his handicaps and became a capable marksman, horseman, and swimmer. He was educated by a tutor and began military training as a young child. At age ten, Wilhelm was made a second lieutenant— five years before he enrolled in the gymnasium, Germany's high school. In 1877, at the age of eighteen, he entered active duty in the army, but served for only a year. Later in the year he entered the University of Bonn and was promoted to first lieutenant.

Kaiser Wilhelm. In early 1888, upon the death of Wilhelm I (Wilhelm's grandfather), Crown Prince Friedrich became king of

▲ Wilhelm II

Event: Leading Europe into World War I.

Role: Wilhelm II, known also as William II or Kaiser Wilhelm, was the third and last emperor of Germany. Trained for military service and international diplomacy, he nonetheless pursued policies that contributed to the outbreak of World War I. Once the war began, however, he remained largely in the background, only occasionally intervening in the German decision-making process.

Prussia and kaiser of the German Reich (state). But he reigned only a few months before dying of throat cancer. On June 15, Wilhelm succeeded his father as Kaiser Wilhelm II. The new emperor seemed determined to take full control of the German empire. He was supported by his admiring subjects, who were captivated by his powerful speeches about finding Germany's "place in the sun." He was, nevertheless, a timid and indecisive ruler, occasionally given to irrational behavior aimed more at satisfying his ambitions than aiding his country.

One of the kaiser's first acts was to dismiss Otto von Bismarck, the chancellor who had dominated German policy since 1862. Bismarck and Wilhelm began quarreling over foreign and domestic policies soon after Wilhelm took office. Bismarck was forced to resign in 1890; the kaiser boasted, "The duty of watchkeeping officer in the ship of state has devolved on me. The course remains as it was: Full steam ahead" (Wilhelm in Kürenberg, pp. 101-02).

Despite promises that he would continue to pursue Bismarck's objectives for Germany, Wilhelm immediately began to alter the course set by the former chancellor. A cornerstone of Bismarck's policy had been maintaining friendly relations with Russia. In 1890 Wilhelm, after consulting with his ministers, decided to allow Bismarck's secret pact of nonaggression with Russia to lapse. Wilhelm had become convinced that Russia might leak news of the pact, which would endanger Germany's alliance with the "Dual Monarchy" of Austria-Hungary. (A monarchy is a government in which a hereditary chief of state with life tenure, like a king or emperor, holds power exclusively.) Bismarck called Wilhelm's decision "an unparalleled mistake" (Kürenberg, p. 105); events would proved him right. Russia, no longer bound to Germany, made an alliance with Germany's potential enemy, France. The kaiser's half-hearted attempts to correct his error by effecting another nonaggression pact with Russia in following years came to nothing.

Searching for world influence. Wilhelm was deeply committed to making Germany a world power. He therefore continued a policy started by Bismarck of seeking economic

▲ Kaiser Wilhelm II was supported by his admiring subjects, who were captivated by his powerful speeches about finding Germany's "place in the sun." He was, nevertheless, a timid and indecisive ruler.

and political involvement around the world. During Wilhelm's reign, Germany had some success with its *Weltpolitik* (world politics). German overseas trade, especially with Latin America, the Far East, and the British Empire, grew rapidly. Germany sent military advisers to the Ottoman Empire to overhaul the

179

▲ Otto von Bismarck, whom Wilhelm dismissed as German chancellor in 1890. The alliances Bismarck forged had held the threat of large-scale war at bay until the twentieth century.

Ottoman military, and a German company began building a railroad between Berlin and Baghdad (now in Iraq). In the late 1890s, Germany acquired territory in China. And in a deal with England that was unpopular with his subjects, Wilhelm traded the African island of Zanzibar for the barren North Sea island Helgoland. During both world wars, Germany would turn Helgoland into a fortress that would successfully protect the North Sea Coast from attack.

▲ Wilhelm (center) observing army maneuvers just before the outbreak of World War I; Wilhelm created an atmosphere of tension in Europe, which was ripe for war.

Despite these successes, the kaiser's *Weltpolitik* lacked a long-term strategy and clearly defined objectives. Moreover, Wilhelm often meddled in events that did not concern Germany; for example, he sent a telegram to South African president Paul Kruger congratulating him on defeating an expedition of British adventurers in 1895. The "Kruger Telegram" strained relations between Germany and England.

Enlarging the navy. And in another major departure from the course set by Bismarck, the kaiser began to beef up the navy. Bismarck had seen Germany's military as a defensive unit; Wilhelm viewed a strong navy as an essential component of his *Weltpolitik*. He blustered about making Germany a great naval power and ruling the waves. In 1897 he put Admiral Alfred von Tirpitz in charge of the navy. Tirpitz, too, believed that a great power should have a large navy and hoped to challenge England's naval supremacy. A more powerful navy, it was believed, would force England to bow to German political demands. As it turned out, the buildup of the German navy had the opposite effect on England.

Watching the German navy grow, England, which depended on sea power for its survival, became increasingly alarmed and began to take countermeasures. It began concentrating naval forces in its home waters in 1904 and soon afterward drew closer to France and Russia. Germany increasingly faced the prospect of "encirclement," which Bismarck had feared. Wilhelm had created an atmosphere of tension in Europe, which was thus ripe for war.

Participation:
Leading Europe Into World War I

The assassination of the archduke. On June 28, 1914, Archduke Francis Ferdinand, heir to the throne of Austria-Hungary, was assassinated in Sarajevo by a Bosnian Serb. (Bosnia was then a part of Austria-Hungary.) This act set in motion a chain of events that led to World War I. As a nation, Serbia, located in southeast Europe, had nothing to do with the assassination. Nevertheless, the act heightened Austria-Hungary's suspicions that Serbia was plotting to take over the Slavic regions of Austria-Hungary in hopes of creating a much larger, and, therefore, more threatening Serbia. Russia, Serbia's ally, it was imagined, would support Serbia's claim to Austro-Hungarian territory.

The assassination inspired heated debate among Austria-Hungary's leaders. The nation's ruler, Kaiser Franz Josef, was reluctant to go to war with Serbia. Others, such as the foreign minister, Count Berchtold, wanted to use the assassination as an excuse to launch a campaign to crush Serbia, which had long been a thorn in Austria-Hungary's side due to threats of territorial expansion. He argued that the murder of the archduke would thus be avenged and external threat to the Dual Monarchy removed.

Wilhelm supports war. Wilhelm, who remarked that "Serbia, with her murderers and bandits, must receive condign [deserved] punishment" (Wilhelm in Kürenberg, p. 299), encouraged Austria-Hungary to launch a punitive war on Serbia and offered to back the Dual Monarchy should Russia interfere. The German kaiser and his chancellor, Theobald von Bethmann-Hollweg, believed that Russia, still recovering from defeat in the Russo-Japanese War, would not enter the conflict. The German leaders reasoned that an Austro-Hungarian victory over Serbia would weaken a strong Russian ally, reduce Russian influence in the Balkan states and ease the threat to the Slavic territories by both Austria-Hungary and Germany. It would also reduce the likelihood of encirclement and perhaps lead to increased political and economic opportunities for Germany in the Balkan states and the Middle East. Once again, however, events would prove Wilhelm wrong.

Russia began to prepare for war. After Austria-Hungary had ignored Serbian objections in 1908 and annexed Bosnia, Germany stepped in to prevent Russia from coming to Serbia's aid. Russia,

The Balkan States

The Balkan nations are a collection of small states—Serbia, Bosnia, Herzegovina, Montenegro, and Greece among them—located on or near the peninsula that is surrounded by the Adriatic, Mediterranean, and Black Seas in North Central Europe. At the beginning of the twentieth century, these nations were fighting with one another but had opposed takeovers by larger nations. But in 1908 Austria-Hungary took over Bosnia and Herzegovina. This angered Serbia; it had hoped to annex the two small states with which it shared a common Slavic heritage. Russia also had a large Slavic population and was a strong supporter of Serbia. When Russia threatened Austria-Hungary over the takeover, that nation's ally, Germany, threatened to protect Austria-Hungary with its military might. Germany had long built its foreign policy around avoiding being surrounded by hostile nations. A large Slavic union of Russian and Balkan states would be such a threat.

Slavic people in Bosnia—the Bosnian Serbs—resented the takeover by Austria-Hungary. The resentment festered until 1914, when it resulted in the start of World War I.

also concerned with its status as a world power, was not about to desert its ally again and face yet another blow to its prestige.

After the assassination of Archduke Ferdinand, Austria-Hungary sent Serbia an ultimatum; it called upon Serbia to curb anti-Austrian propaganda (propaganda is selected information, true or false, that is promoted with the aim of persuading people to adopt a particular belief) and to suppress subversive groups that might incite riots and demonstrations against the Dual Monarchy. Austro-Hungarian leaders seemed to hope that the Serbs would reject the ultimatum and thus give them an excuse to invade Serbia. Serbia, however, accepted the ultimatum—except for a provision allowing Austro-Hungarian officials to enter Serbia to find and punish the assassin or assassins.

On July 28, 1914, Wilhelm received word of Serbia's response to Austria-Hungary's ultimatum. He agreed that it satisfied Austria-Hungary's demands, and he could therefore see no reason for the Dual Monarchy to go to war. But he did not share this opinion with his allies and did nothing to persuade them to keep the peace. Despite Serbia's agreement to meet the monarchy's demands, Austria-Hungary declared war on Serbia later that day.

Russia immediately began to mobilize its forces in defense of Serbia, calling for assistance from its allies. France issued a proclamation that it would stand by any Russian action. At last Kaiser Wilhelm telegraphed appeals for peace to the czar of Russia, to no avail. On August 1, Germany began to mobilize. Wilhelm remarked, "I can do no more" (Kürenberg, p. 303). In fact, he had done much to encourage Austria-Hungary and too little too late to avoid war. Finally, Germany declared war on Russia.

The Kaiser's war plan. German war plans called for first crushing France, Russia's key ally, in an attack through Luxembourg and Belgium, and then sending the bulk of the German armed forces eastward to meet the Russians. When the war began, Germany sent troops into neutral Luxembourg and Belgium to outflank the French forces. But the kaiser and his advisers had not planned on the next event: Great Britain used the violation of Belgium and Luxembourg as a reason to enter the war.

(More likely, Britain was intervening to pursue its own international policy to prevent any single power from dominating Europe.)

England, France, and Russia (the Allies) would eventually be joined by many other nations in waging war against Germany and its partners. Belgium put up a remarkable resistance to the German invasion and was soon joined by British forces. German forces were thus slowed in their advance into France; they were ultimately defeated by the French army at the Battle of the Marne. This upset German plans to quickly eliminate France from the war, which soon became a stalemate.

During much of the war—known then and until World War II simply as the Great War—the kaiser withdrew into the background and generally refrained from interfering in military operations. He would occasionally make largely ceremonial visits to Supreme War Headquarters and give pep talks to the soldiers on the front lines. He did, however, approve German strategies that eventually resulted in defeat.

In late 1914, Germany began sending submarines to attack Allied merchant ships. The move was in response to a British blockade of German North Sea ports, but when the campaign resulted in the sinking of several American vessels (particularly a fatal attack on the ocean liner *Lusitania),* the United States threatened to come into the war on the side of the Allies. Chancellor von Bethmann-Hollweg was then able to enlist the kaiser's support in restricting submarine action. This about-face became German policy for a short time over the objections of military leaders and much of the German public. In 1916 Wilhelm put two powerful generals, Paul von Hindenburg and Erich Ludendorff, in charge of military operations, and Bethmann-Hollweg's power began to wane.

Hindenburg and Ludendorff opposed Bethmann-Hollweg's moderate policies. They argued that the submarine activity was necessary for a German victory, which would result in large territorial gains for the Reich. Disregarding the danger of involving the United States, they argued that a strong submarine campaign

In the summer of 1917, the two German generals, Ludendorff and Hindenburg, established a virtual dictatorship over Germany. At first they were successful in the war; the faltering czarist government in Russia was forced to yield to Germany vast stretches of Russian land. The generals then launched a massive offensive on the western front (France and Belgium). This failed, in part because of the large numbers of new troops coming from America.

The Germans were now on the defensive, and on August 14, the kaiser, seeing no hope of victory, decided to ask for an armistice. Ludendorff opposed this move, and Wilhelm, who had already surrendered much of his power to the two generals, went along. But after Bulgaria surrendered to the Allies in September 1918, Ludendorff changed his mind, ordering an end to submarine warfare and calling on the kaiser to make peace. The German people were frustrated and weary of war. Socialists (proponents of collective or government ownership and administration of the means of production [factories, etc.] and distribution of goods) instigated strikes and mutinies. There were even reports of soldiers in the field sitting down to discuss whether or not to follow their officers' orders.

could knock England out of the war before the United States could effectively respond.

At a high-level meeting in January 1917, Hindenburg and Ludendorff, along with the German admirals, convinced the kaiser to override Bethmann-Hollweg's objections and adopt a policy of unrestricted submarine warfare. German submarines would be ordered to attack neutral as well as Allied shipping. Shortly after this decision, the United States entered the war. By this time, Wilhelm was nearly powerless, having lost much of his control to the German military.

Defeat. With defeat certain, the German press called for the kaiser to abdicate. Wilhelm, however, stood fast. Soon Austria-Hungary had surrendered to the Allies, and a mutiny struck the German navy. Rebellion, led by socialists and the more radical communists, spread throughout the country. At Hindenburg's suggestion, Wilhelm fled to exile in Holland on November 9. Two days later, Germany surrendered. Wilhelm announced his abdication shortly thereafter.

Aftermath

After Wilhelm's flight to Holland, the Allies demanded that he be turned over to them to be tried as a war criminal. Holland refused to comply. In January 1920, some American soldiers attempted to kidnap Wilhelm and turn him over to the Allies. They talked their way into the house where the former kaiser was staying, but the owners of the house became suspicious and called the Dutch police. Wilhelm eventually settled in the town of Doorn. There he wrote his autobiography, as well as a book defending Germany against Allied charges that it alone was responsible for starting World War I.

In 1933 Adolf Hitler came to power in Germany and Wilhelm's son, Prince August Wilhelm, joined Hitler's Nazi party. Kaiser Wilhelm disagreed with Hitler's anti-Jewish campaigns, and during World War II he privately considered the Gestapo (Nazi secret police) and concentration camps (centers of forced labor and human extermination) a disgrace to Germany. Still, fearing for the safety of his relatives in Germany, he made no comment on Hitler's policies.

The kaiser witnessed Germany's victories in Poland and Western Europe at the start of World War II. But he believed Germany would eventually be defeated due to its lack of a navy. (The German armed forces had been largely dismantled after World War I.) On June 4, 1941, less than three weeks before Hitler launched his invasion of the Soviet Union, Kaiser Wilhelm died of pneumonia; he would not live to see Germany defeated in a second world war.

For More Information

Art, Robert. *The Influence of Foreign Policy on Seapower: New Weapons and Weltpolitik in Wilhelminian Germany.* Beverly Hills, California: Sage Publications, 1973.

Gilbert, Martin. *The First World War.* New York: Henry Holt, 1994.

Hillgruber, Andreas. *Germany and the Two World Wars.* Translated by William C. Kirby. Cambridge, Massachusetts: Harvard University Press, 1981.

Kürenberg, Joachim von. *The Kaiser.* Translated by H. T. Russell and Herta Hagen. New York: Simon and Schuster, 1955.

Kurtz, Harold. *The Second Reich.* New York: American Heritage Press, 1970.

May, Ernest R. *The World War and American Isolation.* Cambridge, Massachusetts: Harvard University Press, 1959.

Ramm, Agatha. *Germany, 1789-1919.* London: Methuen, 1967.

Jeannette Rankin

1880-1973

Personal Background

Early life. Jeannette Rankin was born June 11, 1880, on a ranch near Missoula, Montana. Her father, a wealthy land developer and rancher, had immigrated to Montana from Canada.

Jeannette was an adventurous and intelligent child. Although she disliked school and was bored by the memorization that comprised the bulk of study at that time, she was able to learn rapidly; she was equally quick to pick up skills outside of school. She learned to ride and care for horses at an early age. She also became an expert seamstress and dressmaker. By herself, she once constructed a plank sidewalk in front of some buildings her father owned in downtown Missoula.

In 1898 Rankin entered the University of Montana. She was an average student, managing to earn her bachelor of science in the customary four years. Still, she was not well prepared for life after college. Upon graduation she began to cast about for a career. In the early twentieth century, women, even those with college degrees, had a very limited range of career opportunities. One of the available careers was teaching, and Rankin taught elementary school for a short time—until she decided that the classroom was too confining. As she struggled to find rewarding work, she became an apprentice dressmaker, then took a correspondence course in furniture-making. All of these proved to be false starts.

▲ **Jeannette Rankin**

Event: Opposing World War I.

Role: Jeannette Rankin was elected to serve in the U.S. Congress in 1916—the first woman to take a seat in the legislature. In Congress she voted against a resolution calling for a declaration of war against Germany. Reelected in 1940, she again opposed war—this time against Japan. Rankin remained an activist for peace and social reform until her death.

Social awareness. In 1904 Rankin left Montana for the first time, to visit her brother Wellington, a student at Harvard University. The city of Boston was nearby, and she was shocked by the poverty and misery of the city's slums. The visit resulted in her beginning to read the writings of social reformers. Her growing awareness of social problems helped her make a decision to become a social worker. Rankin took a job in a settlement house (an institution providing various community services, especially to large city populations) in San Francisco. But she soon left to enroll in the New York School of Philanthropy (now the Columbia University School of Social Work). She continued her formal education at the University of Washington, studying economics, public speaking, and sociology.

Women's suffrage. During the first years of the twentieth century, there was an increasing demand by women for the right to vote. Rankin soon became involved in a campaign favoring a ballot initiative in Washington State that would give women this right. At first her involvement was routine—distributing posters, stuffing envelopes, and the like. But when campaign leaders became aware of her talents as a speaker and organizer, they sent Rankin around the state to enlist voter support. From this experience, she learned that a successful political campaign requires, among other elements, local committees, public opinion surveys, and a canvassing of voters (a personal solicitation of votes). The campaign she organized was successful; in November 1910, the voters of Washington approved a women's suffrage (voting rights) measure.

Shortly thereafter, Rankin learned that a women's suffrage amendment was to be introduced in the Montana state legislature. She returned to her home state to organize the Equal Franchise Society, through which she worked for passage of the amendment. (The term *franchise* refers here to the right to vote.) When other efforts seemed to be fading, she spoke directly to the state legislature about the issue. Although the amendment failed by a narrow margin, Rankin had helped to firmly establish the women's suffrage movement in Montana. After this initial campaign, she became a professional activist for suffrage and reform groups around the country. Soon Rankin became field secretary for the National Woman Suffrage Association.

Meanwhile, efforts to pass the suffrage amendment in Montana continued. Rankin traveled around the state and organized pro-suffrage committees in each county. She was very successful as a spokesperson, lobbyist, and organizer. The amendment was finally approved by the legislature in 1913 and then submitted to the voters, who approved it the following year.

Participation: Opposing World War I

First woman in Congress. After her success in Montana, Rankin decided to take a vacation abroad. World War I was just beginning, so travel in Europe was out of the question. Instead, she chose to visit New Zealand, in part because women there already had the right to vote. In New Zealand, Rankin took a job as a seamstress in order to help pay for the trip. This undertaking provided her with the time to think about her life and make decisions about her accomplishments and ambitions. The working vacation helped her decide to return to Montana and run for Congress.

Encouraged by her brother, Wellington, now a lawyer, Rankin announced her intention to run as a Republican candidate for a congressional seat. She won the Republican nomination easily over seven men; many women Democrats crossed party lines to vote for her.

In 1916 Montana had such a small population that two congressional seats represented all the state's voters. Would-be representatives had to gather votes from all over the state. Wellington managed Rankin's campaign, and her four sisters also campaigned for her. Rankin traveled throughout the state by car and train, making campaign appearances at factory gates and union halls. Her campaign platform called for national women's suffrage, child labor legislation, and other social reforms.

Among these reforms, Rankin favored prohibition of alcoholic beverages, though knowing Montana's character as a frontier state, she wisely spoke little about this position. Despite opposition from powerful business interests who opposed reform, and from liquor interests who feared prohibition, Rankin was elected to Congress. She was the only Republican winner in Montana that election; Woodrow Wilson, a Democrat, carried the state in the presidential election, and Democrats won the races for governor and for the U.S. Senate.

Antiwar activist. Rankin had hoped to use Congress as a forum to push for women's suffrage and social reform. By the time she took her seat, however, the war in Europe had become the main issue of the day. By the spring of 1917, relations between the United States and Germany had worsened and many in America felt that participation in the war was just a step away. The situation continued to grow more gloomy, and when Congress opened its session on April 2, President Wilson asked for a declaration of war. Rankin's brother supported the president. Well-known suffragists, believing that a "no" vote would damage their campaign, urged her to join in approving the president's request.

A Rankin First

Rankin was the first woman in history to be elected to a national legislature. Her victory made her a national celebrity, and reporters and photographers descended on her home. She made good use of this publicity, however, embarking on a lecture tour that earned her $10,000.

Still, Rankin remained an outspoken opponent of America's entry into the war in Europe; moreover, letters from her supporters in Montana were sixteen to one in opposition to the war.

Early on the morning of April 6, the issue came to a vote in the House of Representatives. A first attempt to support the president was inconclusive. When her turn came to vote on the second roll call, Rankin stated, "I want to stand by my country, but I cannot vote for war. I vote no," then cast the first ever vote by a female representative in Congress (Josephson, p. 77). Nevertheless, the resolution passed the House by a vote of 374 to 50. Later that day, President Wilson issued a declaration of war on Germany.

For the remainder of her term, Rankin pushed for social reform. She offered an amendment calling for equal pay for women, which passed. She also brought about reforms in working conditions at the Bureau of Engraving and Printing, where employees worked long hours at low pay without sick leave or vacation time. By pressuring the secretary of state, Rankin gained an eight-hour work day, sick leaves, paid vacations, and other reforms for bureau workers.

Defeat. Meanwhile, Montana had been divided into two separate congressional districts. Rankin faced a campaign for reelection in a district that now had a Democratic majority. Senators from the state, however, were still elected by the state as a whole. Rankin decided to run for the Senate, which would allow her to campaign as she had two years earlier. But there was a powerful Republican organization at work by then, and Rankin lost the nomination to a candidate supported by this organization.

Rankin then switched parties and ran in the general election as the nominee of the National Party. That party had been founded by socialists (proponents of an economic and political theory advocating collective or government ownership and administration of the means of production [factories, etc.] and distribution of goods), populists (avowed supporters of the common people), and progressives (those believing in moderate political change, especially improvements by governmental action). Both Rankin and the Republican candidate were easily defeated by Thomas J. Walsh, however, a Democrat who had the support of the powerful Anaconda Copper Company.

Suffragettes and the War

Congresswoman Rankin's aide, Belle Fligelman Winestine, recalled visits from leading women's suffrage supporters who told Rankin that by voting against the war, she would turn "suffrage work back twenty years." Rankin, Winestine reported, felt she owed it to the suffrage movement to vote for the war, "but she just didn't see how she could" (from *Jeannette Rankin: The Woman Who Voted No*. Video recording, 1984).

Further Agitation. Rankin left Congress in 1919, determined to devote her life to the antiwar movement. In May 1919, she attended the Women's International Congress for Permanent Peace, which met in Zurich, Switzerland. As a delegate to the congress, she supported resolutions condemning provisions of the Versailles Treaty, which defined conditions for ending World War II; she opposed the heavy reparations the treaty demanded, as well as the seemingly arbitrary drawing of new national borders in Europe. Rankin remained an active member of the Women's International League for Peace and Freedom for the rest of her life.

Between wars. In 1923 Rankin purchased a farm in Georgia. From there she worked for several groups throughout the 1920s and 1930s promoting peace and social reform. Rankin supported international peace efforts through such institutions as the

International Court of Justice. She worked with the General Disarmament Conference and the London Naval Conference to control the accumulation and distribution of weapons. Rankin was also a champion of the Kellogg-Briand Pact of 1928, a bold attempt to outlaw war drawn up by America's secretary of state, Frank Kellogg, and France's foreign minister, Aristide Briand. The measure was accepted by sixty-three nations. It renounced war as an instrument of national policy.

In the United States, Rankin campaigned against an enlarged navy and supported those who wanted to combine air, ground, and naval forces in one defense department. (This was not accomplished until 1947.) Pacifism (a commitment to nonviolent opposition to injustice) was increasingly unpopular during the 1930s as fascist (dictatorial) powers in Germany and Italy became more aggressive. The demand for increased military preparedness in America grew. Membership in pacifist groups such as the Georgia Peace Society, which Rankin had founded, declined, and she came under attack by patriotic organizations such as the American Legion.

Nevertheless, Rankin continued in her efforts for peace, proposing that America avoid intervention abroad. After President Franklin Roosevelt spoke in Chicago in 1937, suggesting that peace-loving nations place a "quarantine" around certain unnamed powers that threatened civilization, Rankin went on a tour opposing action abroad, during which she made 149 speeches and 14 radio broadcasts.

In 1939, believing that she needed a more effective forum, Rankin returned to Montana and prepared to run for another term in Congress. The following year she mounted a powerful campaign that included speaking to the students of fifty-two of the fifty-five high schools in her district. With support from national leaders, she defeated Democrat and incumbent (meaning already

The Treaty of Versailles

Article 231 of the Treaty of Versailles became known as the War Guilt Clause. It laid the full blame for starting World War I, and therefore most of the responsibility of paying all its costs, upon Germany and Austria. Germany lost some land (the Alsace and Lorraine areas) to France and was forced to relinquish more to the new nation of Poland. As a result of the Treaty of Versailles, Finland, Latvia, Estonia, Poland, Czechoslovakia, Austria, Romania, Hungary, Bulgaria, Russia, and Yugoslavia were all redesigned or created as completely new nations.

▲ Rankin photographed in June 1932 before leaving on a speaking tour in support of peace; pacifism grew increasingly unpopular during the 1930s as fascist powers in Germany and Italy became more aggressive.

occupying the office) congressman James O'Connor by more than nine thousand votes.

World War II. As was the case when she was first sent to the legislature, Rankin returned to Congress at a time when the nation was moving toward war. German leader Adolf Hitler's soldiers had invaded Czechoslovakia and Poland in 1939 and were now opposed by Britain and France. America supported Britain and France with supplies and weapons. Rankin nevertheless introduced legislation to prevent American entry into battle. She proposed that congressional approval be required before American troops could be sent overseas, and that any declaration of war be put to a popular vote. But war fever was already raging, and her efforts came to nothing.

On December 8, 1941, one day after the Japanese bombed Pearl Harbor, Roosevelt called Congress into joint session to consider a declaration of war against Japan. Rankin cast the only vote against the resolution. After the vote, she was booed, cursed, and threatened and had to be escorted back to her office by the police. In the following weeks she received a flood of hate mail from the people of Montana and elsewhere.

Rankin chose not to run for reelection. On December 8, 1942, a year after the passage of the declaration of war, she delivered a speech in Congress defending her decision to vote against the war and raising questions about "certain activities" that had led to the Pearl Harbor attack. Rankin suggested that Roosevelt had deliberately taken steps to bring the country into war. She charged that Roosevelt, at British prime minister Winston Churchill's suggestion, had issued a secret ultimatum to Japan demanding that the Japanese refrain from invading "the white empires of the Orient." When the Japanese rejected this ultimatum, said Rankin, Roosevelt imposed an embargo on the sale of scrap iron and petroleum to Japan, which cut off "virtually everything required by the civilian population" of Japan. "It was the sending of this ultimatum," insisted Rankin, "that resulted in the Pearl Harbor attack" (Congressional Record, 1942, pp. 4439-40). Rankin's speech was largely ignored. However, the charges she raised have been echoed by historians ever since.

Aftermath

Continuing peace activism. When her congressional term expired in 1943, Rankin resumed her role as a peace activist, traveling extensively and attending the World Peace Congress in Moscow in 1962 as an observer.

During the 1960s, Rankin became active in the anti-Vietnam War movement. In 1968, at the age of eighty-seven, she led an antiwar march in Washington, D.C. She continued her antiwar activities until 1971. With the conflict in Vietnam winding to a dismal end, Rankin returned to work for social reform.

Rankin advocated changing the American electoral process so that the president would be elected by popular vote rather than by the electoral college (members of which are supposed to cast votes representative of the popular vote). She became a friend and supporter of noted consumer advocate Ralph Nader. Rankin even talked of running for another term in Congress. That faint dream soon faded, however; in 1972 Rankin was diagnosed with an illness that would progressively worsen, making it increasingly difficult for her to speak, swallow, or walk. Nonetheless, she maintained an interest in public affairs, watching closely as the Senate Watergate hearings unfolded before television audiences in the spring of 1973. (Watergate was a series of scandals involving illegal actions by the administration of U.S. president Richard M. Nixon; Nixon resigned from office in August 1974 rather than face impeachment hearings.)

On May 18, 1973, a few weeks short of her ninety-third birthday, Rankin died in her sleep. She had been an unyielding opponent of war and a key advocate of social reform throughout her long life.

For More Information

Josephson, Hannah. *Jeannette Rankin: First Lady in Congress.* Indianapolis: Bobbs-Merrill, 1974.

Regele, Susan Cohen, writer, Ronald Bayley, producer, and Nancy Landgren, director. *Jeannette Rankin: The Woman Who Voted No.* Video recording. Alexandria, Virginia: PBS Video, 1984.

United States of America. *Congressional Record. Proceedings and Debates of the 77th Congress. First Session:* Vol. 87, Part 9: 1941; *Second Session.* Vol. 88, Part 10: 1942. Washington, D.C.: U.S. Government Printing Office, 1941.

Raoul Wallenberg

1912-1947

Personal Background

Birth and early life. Raoul Wallenberg was born in August 1912 in Sweden to a wealthy, well-respected Protestant family. He was born "in caul," which means that part of the birth sac was still covering his head. According to Swedish folklore, this is a sign that a child will be very successful.

Wallenberg's father, also named Raoul, was a naval officer. He was just twenty-three years old when he died of cancer, two months before his son was born. Wallenberg's mother, Maj, was the daughter of a world-renowned neurologist (Per Johann Wising). Maj and Raoul had been married only eight months before he died; she was a widow at twenty-one.

During his early years, Wallenberg was cared for by his mother, his grandfather on his father's side, and a governess. When the boy was six years old, Maj married a hospital administrator named Fredrik von Dardel. Von Dardel accepted Wallenberg as his own son. Together he and Maj would have two children, Nina and Guy. The three children were treated as if they were all of one family.

Gustav Wallenberg, Wallenberg's grandfather, was a successful businessman and ambassador, wealthy and well traveled. He took special care in educating Wallenberg and planning his future.

▲ Raoul Wallenberg

Event: Saving Hungarian Jewry from Nazi extermination.

Role: During World War II, after Germany invaded much of Europe, the German government began to deport Jews in order to exterminate them as part of the Nazi "Final Solution." In 1944, under U.S. pressure, politically neutral Sweden decided to take action. The Swedes sent Raoul Wallenberg to organize a rescue operation to save as many Jews as possible. Through his many talents and extraordinary courage, Wallenberg saved the lives of one hundred thousand Hungarian Jews.

With this encouragement, Wallenberg applied himself to a variety of subjects; he once read the entire thirty-five volumes of Sweden's most comprehensive encyclopedia.

In addition to his thirst for knowledge, young Wallenberg was known for his sense of humor. He often joked that he was lazy, messy, and cowardly when he was actually just the opposite. He sang in the church choir and apparently had a lovely voice. Even as a young man, though, Wallenberg's real passion lay in building and architecture.

World travel. Each summer, grandfather and grandson traveled to a foreign country so that Wallenberg could learn a new language. He became fluent in English, German, Russian, and French. When he was twelve, his grandfather gave him a railroad ticket to travel alone from Stockholm, Sweden, to Istanbul (formerly Constantinople), Turkey. At each stop Wallenberg would hop off the train, returning just in time to catch the parting locomotive, having explored a new city.

Nature Lover

Nature and animals greatly interested Wallenberg. While visiting at his grandfather's friend's farm, he made clear his love of animals. Dogs were kept in kennels on the farm. Feeling sorry for the hounds, Wallenberg decided to set them free. Once they were let out, the dogs went straight for the farmhouse, where they made a huge mess.

After completing high school, Wallenberg worked at the bank that was run by his uncles. That fall he began his mandatory service in the Swedish military. When he was nineteen, Wallenberg traveled to the United States to attend the University of Michigan at Ann Arbor. During his summer breaks he visited Illinois, Arizona, California, and Mexico. He sold pictures that he had drawn to cover travel expenses.

Wallenberg studied architecture and graduated with honors in 1935. Following graduation, he returned to Sweden, where he worked for a short time in Stockholm as an assistant architect. He longed to devote himself fully to architecture. But he had promised his grandfather that he would study commerce and pursue banking, which was, after all, the family business.

Businessman. For six months, Wallenberg lived and worked in Capetown, South Africa. He then accepted a job in

▲ German tanks roll into Hungary, December 15, 1944; the German military planned to remove the Jewish population from Hungary as quickly as possible and send them to concentration camps, where they would be forced into hard labor or sent to their deaths.

Haifa, the main port city of Palestine. There he lived in a Jewish boarding house where he met Jewish refugees who told him of the tremendous suffering they had experienced under Nazi rule.

On returning to Sweden, Wallenberg secured a position at an import-export company. The company's owner was Koloman Lauer, a Hungarian Jew who had escaped Hungary, an ally of Germany, to seek asylum in Sweden. One of the reasons Wallenberg was hired was that he could travel freely in Europe, while Lauer—being a Jew—could not. After eight months, Wallenberg was made a junior partner and director of the company.

In 1942 and 1943, Wallenberg traveled back and forth between Sweden and Hungary on business—and to look in on Lauer's family in Budapest. The Lauer family had difficulty corresponding with each other directly because Hungary, like Germany, enforced strict anti-Jewish laws. Jews, for example, were restricted in the property they could own and the kinds of businesses in which they could participate.

German occupation of Hungary. "Operation Margarethe," the German occupation of Hungary, began on March 17, 1944. It coincided with an intensification of the Nazi's anti-Jewish movement. The German military planned to remove the Jewish population from Hungary as quickly as possible and send them to concentration camps, where they would be forced into hard labor or sent to their deaths.

The World Jewish Congress appealed to the Chief Rabbi of Stockholm and the Swedish Foreign Ministry—Sweden had taken a neutral position during World War II—to do something to save the Jewish people of Hungary. A committee was formed to plan the venture. One committee man was Norbert Masur, the chief rabbi. Masur suggested that Sweden send a diplomat to Hungary to help plan a mission. The Chief Rabbi asked Wallenberg's employer, Lauer, if he knew of a man who could handle such a responsibility. Lauer suggested Wallenberg. The rabbi, however, was not impressed with Wallenberg and claimed that he was too young for such an important task.

Chosen for a rescue mission. In the United States, President Franklin D. Roosevelt had established the War Refugee Board to organize and fund Jewish rescue operations. While the rabbi was still searching for his man, Lauer met the Swedish representative of the War Refugee Board, Iver Olsen, in Sweden.

The Hungarian Jewish Problem

Germany's rapid movements early in World War II had placed Hitler's regime in control of Hungary. The many Jews in Hungary were spread throughout the country and there was a great anti-Jewish sentiment. As the war reached its peak, a Hungarian organization sympathetic to the Germans known as the Arrow Cross systematically tormented Hungarian Jews.

In early 1944, Adolf Eichmann, acting on Hitler's orders, divided Hungary into six precincts in order to systematically round up all Hungarian Jews and transport them to camps to be slaughtered. By mid-1944, three thousand Jews a month were being herded into boxcars each day for their final ride.

Olsen also asked Lauer if he knew of anyone who could go to Hungary to save the Jews. Again Lauer suggested Wallenberg.

Olsen met with Wallenberg and, after spending the entire night with him, was convinced that Wallenberg was right for the assignment. It was agreed that Wallenberg would go to Hungary for two to three months. In this way the United States came to finance the mission of a Swedish diplomat to Hungary.

Participation: Saving Hungarian Jewry From Nazi Extermination

The situation in Hungary. By the time Wallenberg began preparing to leave for Hungary, half of the Jewish population there had already been deported or killed. The remaining Jews—most of them in Budapest—were required to wear patches with a yellow (six-pointed) Star of David, a Jewish symbol, so that they could be identified easily. They lived in ghettos and were forbidden to leave their homes. Nor were the Jews of Budapest allowed to have telephones, radios, bicycles, or cars. Without communication or transportation, they could not organize themselves against the Germans. Short supplies of food left many in a weakened condition. The Hungarian Jews were nearly helpless.

A Plan to Marry

When Wallenberg accepted his assignment in Budapest, Hungary, he planned on being gone for two to three months. A few days before he decided to go, he proposed marriage to his eighteen-year-old girlfriend, Jeannette von Heidenstam, who later became a Swedish television star. Although she never officially said no, she remarked that she was perhaps too young to get married. Wallenberg was thirty-one at the time.

Wallenberg arrived in Budapest as an officer of the Swedish diplomatic corps. The position gave him protection as a diplomat, and American money allowed him to hire a staff of his choosing. Wallenberg and his staff established hospitals, nurseries, and soup kitchens for the persecuted Jews.

The passport. One of the first things Wallenberg did when he got to Budapest was to design a fake Swedish passport. It was printed in yellow and blue ink with official-looking government seals, which made it appear very impressive. Such passports became the most effective means Wallenberg had of saving lives.

Because the passports looked so authentic, and because Wallenberg was a very persuasive person, he convinced the Nazis to let thousands of Jews go to Sweden and live under the protection of the Swedish government. Wallenberg often threatened German soldiers, saying that they would be tried as war criminals if they did not honor the Swedish passports. This tactic was almost always effective.

By the end of his three-month assignment, Wallenberg and his staff had saved many Jewish lives by distributing passports and bribing and blackmailing officials. The entire Swedish staff had risked life and limb in various ways to combat the Final Solution (the Nazi plan to kill all Jews and people of other races Hitler thought undesirable, including Slavs). At the end of September 1944, Wallenberg thought that he would soon be going home.

At about this time, Hungary's head of state, Miklós Horthy, began to feel that Germany and its allies were going to lose the war. Wallenberg helped persuade Horthy to break away from Germany and sign a truce with Russia. Horthy used Hungarian radio to broadcast the news that, for Hungary, the war was over. The Jews rejoiced. But Horthy had not been prepared for the German reaction to his plan.

About thirty minutes after Horthy's peace announcement, the Germans and the fascist (totalitarian) Hungarian organization the Arrow Cross seized control of Budapest. They named a new head of state—Ferenc Szalasi, the leader of the Arrow Cross. Immediately the situation became even more dire for the Jews; Wallenberg realized that his mission was not yet over.

The members of the Arrow Cross formed a mob that, among other acts of violence, murdered Jews openly in Budapest. At the same time, orders had come from Germany to destroy the Hungarian Jewish population once and for all. Jews were to be rounded up and sent to concentration camps by foot and on trains. Wallenberg redoubled his efforts in the face of this increased persecution, though he, too, was now in greater personal danger. He began to bring passports, food, clothes, and medicine to the Jews up and down the railway line, reaching many just as they prepared to board trains to their deaths. He and his colleagues rescued about two thousand people this way.

Success. Wallenberg and his staff, now numbering to more than four hundred—mostly Hungarian Jews given asylum by Sweden—continued their work. Even so, the Germans came close to eliminating the Jewish population of Hungary many times during the war. Wallenberg used every method available to thwart these efforts. Using bribes and spies, he was able to get details on Arrow Cross and Nazi plans to deport Jews. He protested these actions with letters to the Foreign Ministry of Hungary and personal meetings with government and military officials.

Toward the end of 1944, conditions in Budapest grew even more chaotic. Inside the city, Arrow Cross thugs continued to act ruthlessly. Moreover, Budapest was being attacked at all hours by the Allied forces (of Great Britain, the United States, and their partners). Per Anger, Wallenberg's fellow diplomat, encouraged him to move out of the city to safer surroundings, but Wallenberg refused. When Anger asked him if he was afraid, Wallenberg replied:

> It is frightening at times, but I have no choice. I have taken upon myself this mission and I would never be able to return to Stockholm without knowing that I've done everything that stands in a man's power to rescue as many Jews as possible. (Bierman, p. 114)

As a precaution, however, Wallenberg rarely slept in the same apartment for more than one night, if he slept at all. Adolf Eichmann, the Nazi in charge of the deportation of Jews, had made at least two attempts to have him killed and had told Wallenberg personally that he would try again.

Still, Wallenberg achieved what seemed impossible during these times. One technique was particularly effective: just as the Arrow Cross or Nazis were lining people up at the train stations to send them to their deaths, Wallenberg would arrive carrying a thick, official-looking book. He would demand to speak with anyone who had a Swedish passport. Hundreds would line up to see him. Anyone with any kind of paper with a name on it was announced to be holding a Swedish passport, the name was entered in the official book, and the person was sent back to the safe homes Wallenberg had bought from Hungarian and German officials.

Aftermath

In January 1945, two days before the Russians entered Budapest and effectively liberated Hungary from Nazi control, there were 69,000 Jews in the General Ghetto, 25,000 in the International Ghetto, and another 25,000 in hiding across town in monasteries, convents, churches, and homes of non-Jews. In total, almost 120,000 Hungarian Jews had survived the Nazi Holocaust; about 100,000 of them owed their lives to Raoul Wallenberg.

Back in November 1944, Wallenberg had begun to plan for the recovery of Hungary's Jewish community. He assigned a young Jewish economist (Rezso Müller) to draft a plan that would take effect after the Germans had been defeated. It contained provisions for finding missing persons, reuniting families, establishing homes for orphans, issuing emergency food supplies, preparing housing, and providing medical care. The plan also called for an information service, reestablishment of businesses, and development of employment opportunities.

When Russia took control of Hungary, the Nazis either fled to Germany or were taken prisoner. Wallenberg decided to present his recovery plan to the Hungarian Provincial Government based in Debrecen. Knowing that the 120-mile trip to Debrecen would be a dangerous journey, Wallenberg contacted a Russian major, seeking some sort of protection.

Once they met, the major barely left Wallenberg's side. Wallenberg joked that it was not clear whether the major was simply protecting him or holding him prisoner. He set off for Debrecen with great optimist, certain that he would be able to deliver his recovery plan and return to Sweden. It was not to be.

Arrest. En route to Debrecen, Wallenberg was taken into custody by the Russian secret service. A Russian agent, working undercover in the Red Cross, had been observing Wallenberg during much of his rescue mission. Because the mission had been funded by the United States and because Wallenberg had been so successful in negotiating with the Germans, the Russians could not believe that he was in Hungary just to save Jews; they were convinced that Wallenberg was a spy, working as a double agent for the United States and England—and for Germany.

In January 1945, when the Swedish government asked about Wallenberg's whereabouts, the Russians replied that Wallenberg was safely in their custody. Later, they changed their story, claiming that Wallenberg had been killed by Germans or the Arrow Cross in Hungary. Many years later, the Russians changed their tune yet again, after persistent investigation of Wallenberg's disappearance by the Swedish government; they claimed that Wallenberg had died of a heart attack in prison in 1947. For fifty years the Russians kept Wallenberg's fate a secret.

In the wake of the collapse of the Soviet Union, the truth about Wallenberg finally surfaced: Wallenberg had been placed in a Russian prison immediately after he was captured in January 1945. For over two years, the Russians tortured him, trying to make him become a Russian agent. Wallenberg never submitted. In 1947 he was killed by the Russian secret service.

For More Information

Bierman, John. *Righteous Gentile: The Story of Raoul Wallenberg, Missing Hero of the Holocaust.* New York: Viking, 1981.

Levai, Jeno. *Raoul Wallenberg: His Remarkable Life, Heroic Battles and the Secret of his Mysterious Disappearance.* Melbourne: White Ant Occasional Printing, 1989.

Marton, Kati. "The Liquidation of Raoul Wallenberg: At Last, the True Story Is Out." *Washington Post,* 22 January 1995, Outlook Section, pp. 1, 4.

Werbell, Frederick E., and Thurston Clark. *Lost Hero: The Mystery of Raoul Wallenberg.* New York: McGraw-Hill, 1982.

Charles de Gaulle

1890-1970

Personal Background

Destined for military life. Charles de Gaulle was born in Lille in northern France, near the Belgian border, on November 22, 1890. He was the son of a teacher but did not prove to be an exceptional student. De Gaulle did, however, even as a young child, have a powerful memory. This helped him do well in the subjects that interested him—history, literature, and philosophy. Still, even in his pre-teens, his favorite activity was playing at soldiering.

De Gaulle reached his teenage years just as France's third attempt at a republic seemed to be deteriorating. For thirty years the region had been divided between those who continued to favor a republic and those of the noble class still hoping for a monarchy. (The term *republic* signifies a government wherein power rests in a body of citizens entitled to vote and which exercises that power through elected officers who govern according to law; a monarchy is a government in which a hereditary chief of state with life tenure, like a king or emperor, holds power exclusively.) Meanwhile, France's neighbors increasingly threatened French security. Amid this turmoil, de Gaulle recognized that most of the institutions of the Third Republic appeared weak. Only the Catholic Church and the army seemed to be strong and stable. He decided to pursue a career in the army.

▲ Charles de Gaulle

Event: Leading French resistance in World War II.

Role: During the early days of World War II, Charles de Gaulle commanded an armored unit in the French army and later served in the government. After fleeing to London when initial French resistance collapsed in 1940, de Gaulle organized the Free French, who fought with the Allies opposing the German-Italian Axis.

After attending a preparatory school, de Gaulle was prepared to fulfill the basic requirement for entrance to the national military academy of Saint-Cyr. All would-be enrollees were required to first spend a year in the service. De Gaulle enlisted in the army in October 1909, then entered Saint-Cyr a year later. He graduated from the academy in 1912. After graduating, de Gaulle enlisted in the Thirty-Third Infantry Regiment—the outfit he had joined in 1909—as a sublieutenant. His commanding officer, Colonel Philippe Petain, was impressed by his performance and promoted him to lieutenant.

De Gaulle saw action soon after World War I broke out. He was wounded while fighting in Belgium in 1914 and again in 1915. The next year, after he had recovered, he fought in the Battle of Verdun, during which he was wounded and taken prisoner. He was released by the Germans at the end of the war.

In 1918 de Gaulle joined a Polish cavalry unit (the Polish army was rebuilding after the World War I takeover by Germany and this offered possibilities for military experience and advancement) and was soon back in action, this time against the Russian Bolsheviks. (The Bolsheviks, under the leadership of Lenin, had formed a radical left-wing group in 1917 and had taken over the direction of the Russian Revolution; their doctrines derived from the work of German social theorist Karl Marx and upheld a revolution led by workers and peasants.) De Gaulle took part in the battle to defend Warsaw from the Soviets in 1920, rising to the rank of major. Then, while on leave from his Polish army duty, he married a woman ten years his junior named Yvonne, the daughter of a biscuit manufacturer in Paris. When peace between Poland and the Soviet Union was finally arranged in 1921, de Gaulle returned to France to lecture at Saint-Cyr. He was then admitted to the École Superieur de Guerre, or Higher Military School, to be trained for higher rank.

De Gaulle's instructors at the École Superieur admired his self-confidence and brilliant performance, but they resented his unwillingness to compromise or accept criticism. His tendency to be aloof also bothered them; one officer complained that he behaved like a "king in exile" (Cook, p. 36). This attitude nearly ruined his career. His instructors wanted to give him the lowest possible grade, which would have prevented him from advancing to higher command. However, his old commander and mentor, Philippe Petain, now a field marshal, saw to it that he received the higher grade that was needed for promotion.

Military reformer. In 1932 de Gaulle published a forward-thinking article, later expanded into a book, in which he advocated reforming the French army to emphasize mobile warfare and the use of tanks. His arguments irritated his superiors, who favored a defensive strategy based on the Maginot Line, a system of fixed fortifications along France's eastern border (obsolete before it was completed in 1934, the Maginot Line was easily bypassed by the German mobile advance in World War II). Still, de Gaulle continued writing and training for higher command. In 1938 he was assigned to a tank unit.

Participation:
Leading French Resistance in World War II

France declares war. On September 1, 1939, German forces invaded Poland, and France declared war on Germany. At the time, de Gaulle was commanding an armored unit supporting the Maginot Line defenses. This front remained relatively quiet until May 10, 1940, when the Germans launched a massive assault on Holland, Belgium, Luxembourg, and France. On May 11, de Gaulle was given command of a hastily assembled and ill-prepared armored division. Attacking without air support, they routed a German unit in an engagement north of Paris. The Germans reacted quickly, though, forcing the French to withdraw and holding off another French counterattack. De Gaulle's men were moved to Abbeville in northwestern France, where they made another successful counterattack. Meanwhile, de Gaulle had been promoted to brigadier general.

On June 5, de Gaulle was called to Paris, where Premier Paul Reynaud named him undersecretary of state for national defense. Many government leaders, including the new commander of the army, believed that Germany could not be defeated and wanted to

▲ De Gaulle salutes a sentry at his London headquarters, 1942; after
French resistance collapsed in 1940, de Gaulle organized the Free
French, who fought with the Allies opposing the German-Italian Axis.

make peace at any cost. De Gaulle asked Reynaud to replace the
commander.

Still, the better-prepared German forces pressed into northern France. When they took Paris, de Gaulle urged the French
government to move to North Africa and continue the fight. (At
the outset of the war, French colonies included Morocco, Algeria,
Tunisia, and Equatorial West Africa.) Reynaud, however, delayed

a decision until it was too late. On June 16, his government fell and was replaced by one controlled by the Nazis and led by de Gaulle's old benefactor Petain. De Gaulle fled to London. Under the terms of France's surrender to Germany, Germans occupied northern and western France, including Paris, while the French government under Petain moved to the town of Vichy in south-central France. During the next few years, the Vichy government, as it was called, would cooperate extensively with the Nazis, who, led by Adolf Hitler, controlled Germany.

Government in exile. In London, British prime minister Winston Churchill sought a way to encourage the French to continue fighting against the occupying Germans. He gave de Gaulle permission to use British Broadcasting Corporation (BBC) facilities to make a radio broadcast to France. In a four-minute speech known as the "Call to Honor," de Gaulle told the French people that the war was not lost and that they should continue resistance. He then set up the Provisional French National Committee and attempted to recruit volunteer fighters from among French refugees in England.

But de Gaulle was not well known, and many of the French did not trust him. In addition, his committee was seen as a creation of the British, whose popularity among the French had fallen dramatically. Nonetheless, over the next few months, a trickle of soldiers, a few naval units, and some colonial governments (of nations outside of France but under French control) began rallying to de Gaulle.

In September 1940, de Gaulle's forces, now known as the Free French, attacked the port of Dakar in French West African (now Senegal) with British naval support; they were driven off, however, by pro-Vichy French forces. Nevertheless, the Free French continued to grow, and de Gaulle moved his headquarters to Brazzaville in French Equatorial Africa (now Congo).

Allied frictions. In the spring of 1941, the British and Free French launched an invasion of Syria and Lebanon, which were held by Vichy French forces. To gain a quick surrender from the French, the British commander agreed to allow the Vichy French to return home. De Gaulle opposed this; he thought the British should have given the Vichy troops the opportunity to defect to the Free French. When the British realized that the French soldiers allowed to return to France were taking fifty-two captured British officers with them, they stopped the ships at sea, rescued the officers, and made de Gaulle's offer. Six thousand out of twenty-five thousand Vichy troops chose to join de Gaulle.

De Gaulle's relations with the United States were equally stormy. He resented America's continued recognition of the Vichy government (which was, in fact, the official French government). Then, in December 1941, American officials decided to disable a radio transmitter believed to be sending out information useful to German submarines. This equipment was located on the Vichy-held French islands of Saint-Pierre and Miquelon in the Gulf of St. Lawrence. So as not to offend Vichy, U.S. president Franklin D. Roosevelt and Churchill agreed that Canadian forces and not the Free French should seize the islands and disable the transmitter. De Gaulle agreed to this plan but sent secret orders to Free French naval units to seize the islands. According to his biographer Don Cook, this "wholly unnecessary" confrontation with the United States cost de Gaulle "all hopes of early recognition by Roosevelt and sealed his complete exclusion from the higher political and military counsels of war" (Cook, p. 143).

De Gaulle and the British

Friction between de Gaulle and his British allies continued throughout the war and beyond. The British responded to de Gaulle's frequent public criticism by restricting his movements and denying him use of the BBC. Churchill would later say, "Of all the crosses I have had to bear, the heaviest was the Cross of Lorraine," the double-barred cruciform that the Free French used as their symbol (Churchill in Nixon, p. 41).

For the rest of his life, de Gaulle's relations with the United States would remain cool. His rapport with the British also continued to be chilly, improving only slightly when the Free French won their first victory over the Germans, at Bir Hakeim in Libya in June 1942. In November, however, American and British forces staged Operation Torch, an amphibious (by sea) invasion of French North Africa. De Gaulle's forces were not only excluded from this operation—they weren't even informed of its existence.

Meanwhile, Vichy-French forces were resisting the Operation Torch landings. In order to bring about a cease-fire, the Allies (nations opposing Germany and its partners) made an agreement with Admiral Francois Darlan, the commander of Vichy's armed forces. The deal allowed Darlan to administer the rest of North Africa, while the Allies occupied Morocco and Algeria. This arrangement was denounced by de Gaulle and generated widespread criticism in England and the United States. Darlan's murder, in December 1942, removed a source of embarrassment and ill-feeling among the Allies.

After Darlan was killed, de Gaulle and Henri Giraud, another French general who had fought in Africa, agreed to form the French Committee of National Liberation, in which they would share power. Despite American support for Giraud, de Gaulle soon maneuvered him out of power. De Gaulle then began purging Vichyites who had infiltrated the Free French army. Meanwhile, the all-powerful Gestapo (the Nazi secret state police) hunted down and imprisoned de Gaulle's relatives who remained in France.

De Gaulle and the Free French were not allowed to participate in the Normandy invasion in June 1944, but the general's forces were soon fighting alongside the Allied troops as they moved inland. (The Normandy landing on June 6, 1944—now known as D-Day—began the Allied invasion of Europe. Under the command of U.S. general Dwight D. Eisenhower, ninety thousand British, American, and Canadian troops landed on the beaches of France in one of the most complex feats of organization and supply in history.) On June 14, de Gaulle returned to France for the first time since 1940. As the Allies advanced, de Gaulle ordered Vichy officials replaced by his own followers.

Ruler of France. Allied troops were soon nearing Paris, where Eisenhower hoped to avoid being bogged down in street fighting; he planned to bypass the city and head straight for Germany. Meanwhile, a Communist-led uprising had begun in Paris. De Gaulle was concerned that the Communists would seize control and challenge his power. He threatened to order Free French units to take Paris—which would have considerably disrupted the Allied advance.

▲ De Gaulle returns to a just-liberated Paris, June 14, 1944; as the Allies advanced, de Gaulle ordered Vichy officials replaced by his own followers.

When Eisenhower learned that the Germans were prepared to destroy the city's most famous landmarks, he changed his mind about avoiding Paris; on August 22, he ordered Free French forces to take the French capital. On completing this task, de

Gaulle assumed the role of "President of the Government of the Republic" (Cook, p. 249). In September de Gaulle announced the formation of a provisional government.

To confirm France's status as a great power and to help bring the Communists under control, de Gaulle sought to improve relations with the Soviet Union. He pardoned Communist leader Maurice Thorez, who had deserted the French army during the Battle for France in early 1940 and had fled to Moscow. Although this move brought de Gaulle criticism, Thorez helped de Gaulle to finally bring the Communist militias under control.

Aftermath

War's end. France was not invited to participate in the Yalta conference in February 1945 (which provided for the treatment of a defeated Germany). Nevertheless, at the insistence of the British delegates present, France obtained a favorable position in postwar Europe, including an occupation zone in Germany, a sector in Berlin, and a seat on the Allied Control Council that would administer Germany.

Angered by his exclusion, de Gaulle declined an invitation to meet with Roosevelt in Algiers on his way back to Washington. De Gaulle's snub of the president was not popular with the French people, who considered it rude, and it did nothing to improve his relations with Washington. Franco-American relations did not improve after Roosevelt's death. When de Gaulle ordered French troops to occupy Stuttgart in the American zone in Germany, and later, when he sent troops across the Italian border apparently hoping to grab a slice of northern Italy for France, President Harry Truman forced him to back down by threatening a cutoff of United States aid.

> ## De Gaulle and the Soviet Union
>
> In late 1944, de Gaulle flew to Moscow and met with Soviet leader Joseph Stalin to discuss a treaty of alliance. Nonetheless, he refused Stalin's demand that he recognize the Soviet-sponsored Communist government in Poland. The London-based Polish government-in-exile, after all, had been the first to recognize the Free French during the war; de Gaulle could not embrace its opponent. Stalin eventually dropped this demand, telling de Gaulle, "You play your hand well" (Stalin in Cook, p. 267). The treaty of alliance was signed in December 1944.

Relations between the two countries warmed somewhat after de Gaulle accepted an invitation to visit Truman in Washington in August 1945. Truman promised a $650 million loan to France.

Resignation. At home, de Gaulle's grip on power was growing weaker. Over his objections, the French were planning a constitution that would provide for the "Fourth Republic," which would feature a strong legislature and a weak chief executive. De Gaulle strongly opposed this move. He believed that the lack of a strong executive was one of the major failings of the Third Republic. He also found himself relying increasingly on Communist support to pass legislation that he favored. On January 20, 1946, as the Fourth Republic was born, de Gaulle resigned the presidency of France.

Resisting the Fourth Republic. De Gaulle continued to criticize the Fourth Republic, convinced that it would eventually collapse. In the late 1940s, his supporters set up the Rally for the People of France to influence government through Nazi-style rallies and a paramilitary organization. This movement grew rapidly for a time before collapsing in the early 1950s.

For a while, it looked like the Fourth Republic might succeed. However, by the mid-1950s, unrest in the French colony of Algeria and elsewhere, continued political instability, a fading economy, and squabbling among France's many political factions demonstrated its weakness; de Gaulle's supporters began organizing to bring him back. In 1958 the National Assembly finally turned to de Gaulle in order to head off a military coup.

De Gaulle pushed through a new constitution in 1958, initiating what is known as the Fifth Republic, which restored a strong presidency. He served as president under this constitution—once again obstinate and uncompromising in his dealings with his Allies. Then, in 1968, he was nearly driven from office by a revolt led by leftist students. The next year he resigned, after losing a referendum on reforms he had proposed. He died in 1970.

Still, de Gaulle's legacy lives on. The Fifth Republic has endured, and Jacques Chirac, former mayor of Paris and a Gaullist (a member of the political party named after de Gaulle), was elected president of France in May 1995.

For More Information

Cook, Don. *Charles de Gaulle*. New York: G. P. Putnam's Sons, 1983.

Nixon, Richard. *Leaders*. New York: Warner, 1982.

Weinberg, Gerhard L. *A World in Arms*. New York: Cambridge University Press, 1994.

Bibliography

Baker, David. *The Rocket: The History and Development of Rocket and Missile.* New York: Crown, 1978.

Balflour, Michael. *The Kaiser and His Times.* Boston: Houghton Mifflin, 1964.

Brecht, Bertholt. *Seven Plays by Bertolt Brecht.* Edited by Eric Bentley. New York: Grove Press, 1961.

Buck, Pearl S. *The Man Who Changed China: The Story of Sun Yat-sen.* New York: Random House, 1953.

Burge, Frederica M., and Rinn-Sup Shinn. *China: A Country Study.* United States Secretary of the Army, Washington, D.C., 1981.

Chen, Stephen. *Sun Yat-sen: A Patriot.* New York: John Day, 1946.

Crouch, Tom D. *The Bishop's Boys: A Life of Wilbur and Orville Wright.* New York: Norton, 1989.

De Forest, Lee. *Father of Radio: The Autobiography of Lee De Forest.* Chicago: Wilcox and Follett, 1950.

Demetz, Peter. *A Collection of Critical Essays.* Englewood Cliffs, New Jersey: Prentice-Hall, 1962.

Duma, Andrew. *Marie Curie.* New York: Boatwright, 1991.

Fairbank, John King. *China: A New History.* Cambridge, Massachusetts: Belknap Press, 1992.

Frank, Philip. *Einstein: His Life and Times.* New York: Alfred A. Knopf, 1947.

Frölich, Paul. *Luxemburg, Ideas in Action.* London: Left Book Club, 1940.

Giround, Francois. *Marie Curie. A Life.* New York: Holmes and Maier, 1986.

Hartley, Anthony. *Gaullism: The Rise and Fall of a Political Movement.* New York: Outerbridge and Dienstfray, 1971.

Hoffman, Barresh. *Albert Einstein: Creator and Rebel.* New York: Viking, 1972.

Johnson, Spencer. *The Value of Patience: The Story of the Wright Brothers.* La Jolla: Value Power, 1976.

Josephson, Hannah G. *Jeannette Rankin: First Lady in Congress.* Indianapolis: Bobbs-Merrill, 1974.

La Couture, Jean. *De Gaulle.* New York: Norton, 1990–92.

Lenin, Vladimir Ilyich. *Lenin Reader.* Edited by Stefan T. Possony. Chicago: H. Regnery, 1966.

Levine, Israel E. *Electronic Pioneers: Lee De Forest.* New York: J. Messner, 1964.

BIBLIOGRAPHY

Lewis, Thomas S. W. *Empire of the Air: The Men Who Made Radio.* New York: Edward Burlingame, 1991.

Luxemburg, Rosa. *Reform or Revolution?* Staten Island, New York: Gordon Press, 1973.

Manchester, Harland. *New Trailblazers of Technology.* New York: Charles Scribner's Sons, 1976.

Maurice, Francois. *De Gaulle.* Garden City, New York: Doubleday, 1966.

McMahon, John Robert. *The Wright Brothers: Fathers of Flight.* Boston: Little, Brown, 1930.

Miller, Robert Ryal. *Mexico: A History.* Norman, Oklahoma: University of Oklahoma Press, 1985.

Mitchell, David J. *The Fighting Pankhursts: A Study in Tenacity.* New York: Macmillan, 1967.

Neimark, Anne. *Sigmund Freud: The World Within.* New York: Harcourt Brace, 1976.

Noble, Iris. *Emmeline and Her Daughters.* New York: J. Messner, 1971.

Parker, Barry R. *Einstein's Dream: The Search for a Unified Theory of the Universe.* New York: Planum, 1986.

Parmelin, Helena. *Picasso Plain: An Intimate Portrait.* New York: St. Martin's, 1963.

Payne, Melvin M., editor. *Those Inventive Americans.* Washington, D.C.: National Geographic Society, 1971.

Pflaum, Rosalynd. *Grand Obsession: Marie Curie and Her World.* Garden City: Doubleday, 1989.

Picasso: 75th Anniversary Exhibition. New York: The Museum of Modern Art, 1957.

Quinn, Susan. *Marie Curie: A Life.* New York: Simon and Schuster, 1995.

Quinn, Susan. *Russian Revolution and Leninism or Marxism?,* Westport, Connecticut: Greenwood Press, 1981.

Reed, Robert William. *Marie Curie.* New York: Saturday Review, 1974.

Robinson, John R. *China from the Manchu to Mao, 1699-1976.* New York: Atheneum, 1980.

Sayen, Jamie. *Einstein in America.* New York: Crown, 1985.

Stleinke, Ann E. *Marie Curie and the Discovery of Radium.* New York: Barron's, 1987.

Walsh, John Evangelist. *One Day at Kitty Hawk: The Untold Story of the Wright Brothers.* New York: Crowell, 1975.

Williams, Charles. *The Last Great Frenchman: A Life of General de Gaulle.* New York: John Wiley, 1995.

Index

Bold indicates entries and their page numbers; (ill.) indicates illustrations.

CCRI/LRC

3 1618 00199 9806

WORLD HISTORY

Significant Events and the People Who Shaped Them